Hodder Cambridge Primary

Maths

Learner's Book

Stage 4

Josh Lury

Series editors: Mike Askew and Paul Broadbent

HODDER EDUCATION
AN HACHETTE UK COMPANY

Author acknowledgements

With warm thanks to Jennifer Peek for her help in shaping and developing this title.

The Publisher is extremely grateful to the following schools for their comments and feedback during the development of this series:

Avalon Heights World Private School, Ajman

The Oxford School, Dubai

Al Amana Private School, Sharjah

British International School, Ajman

Wesgreen International School, Sharjah

As Seeb International School, Al Khoud.

Photograph acknowledgements

We would like to thank the following for their permission to reproduce photographs:

p.8 © Telnov Oleksii/Shutterstock; **p.12** © Mearicon/123rf; **p.13** t, c, bl , **p.51** (both), p.131 (all), **p.170** (both) © Hachette UK; **p.13** br © Maks Narodenko/Shutterstock; **p.27** t © Smileus/123rf; **p.27** b © Rostislav Ageev/123rf; **p.33** © Rawpixel.com/Shutterstock; **p.47** © inkcandy/Shutterstock; **p.49** © Alexander Dashewsky/Shutterstock; **p.61** l © Nathapol Boonmangmee/123rf; **p.61** c © Malgorzata Kistryn/123rf; **p.61** r © Ivan Aleshin/123rf; **p.70** © Lucas Vallecillos/VWPics/Alamy Stock Photo; **p.92** © Brux/123rf; **p.115** © Gevision/Shutterstock; **p.118** © Joseph Belanger/123rf; **p.158** © Jeff Gilbert/Alamy Stock Photo

t = top, b = bottom, l = left, r = right, c = centre

Practice test exam-style questions and sample answers are written by the author.

Orders: please contact Hachette UK Distribution, Hely Hutchinson Centre, Milton Road, Didcot, Oxfordshire, OX11 7HH. Telephone: +44 (0)1235 827827. Email education@hachette.co.uk Lines are open from 9 a.m. to 5 p.m., Monday to Friday. You can also order through our website: www.hoddereducation.com

© Josh Lury 2017

Published by Hodder Education

An Hachette UK Company

Carmelite House, 50 Victoria Embankment, London EC4Y 0DZ

Impression number   10

Year   2021

Cover illustration by Steve Evans

Illustrations by Alex van Houwelingen, Vian Oelofsen and DTP Impressions

Typeset in FS Albert 15/17 by DTP Impressions

Printed and bound by CPI Group (UK) Ltd, Croydon, CR0 4YY

A catalogue record for this title is available from the British Library

9781471884375

Contents

Introduction

Explore the picture or problem.
What do you see? What can you find out?

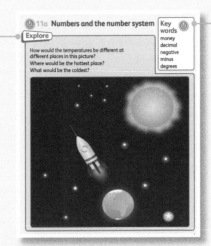

11a Numbers and the number system

Explore

How would the temperatures be different at different places in this picture?
Where would be the hottest place?
What would be the coldest?

Key words
money
decimal
negative
minus
degrees

Key words are in a list for you to learn.

Learn new maths skills with your teacher. Look at the diagrams to help you.

Learn

Where would these numbers go in the Venn diagram?

4 12 9 18 3 21

Multiple of 2   Multiple of 3

A B C

Think of numbers that would not go in A, B or C.

Practise the maths you have learnt. Write any answers in your exercise book.

Practise

1 Copy and complete. The first one has been done for you.

a 13 × 10 = 130   b × 10 = 190   c 450 ÷ 10 =
   23 × 10 =   × 10 = 380   540 ÷ 10 =
   230 × 10 =   × 10 = 3800   + 10 = 36
   235 × 10 =   × 10 = 3840   + 10 = 63

2 Use these digit cards more than once each to make multiplications and divisions. How many solutions can you find? The first one has been done for you.

2 5 0 ×10 ÷10 =   2 5 ×10 ÷ = 2 5 0

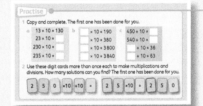

Try this challenge activity to make you think carefully about the maths.

Try this

Choose two amounts that round to $3, but when added, the sum does NOT round to $6.
Write two more solutions.

Think like a mathematician

People sometimes think that $1.5 means $1 and 5 cents. To avoid confusion, use two numbers after the decimal point. $1.5 means $1.50 which is $1 and 50c.

Read these hints and tips to help you **think like a mathematician**.

At the end of each unit try the **self-check** activities. What have you learnt?

Self-check

A **Number patterns**

1 Copy and complete the sequences:
   a 25, 50,   , 100,   , 150
   b 250, 230,   , 190,   ,
   c   ,   , 96, 93, 90
   d 1,   , 41,   , 81,

2 Write 10 more, 100 more and 1 000 more than each number:
   a 1234
   b 4321
   c 4343
   d 1212

B **Multiplication and division**

1 4 × 9 = ?
2 8 × 3 = ?
3 6 × 8 = ?
4 What is double 33?
5 What number doubled is 52?
6 What is the remainder for 89 ÷ 4?
7 If you need 4 eggs to make one cake, how many eggs do you need to make 5 cakes?

Unit 1 Number and problem solving

 1a Place value and decimals

Key words

Key words
ten thousand
digit
numeral
place value
partition

Explore

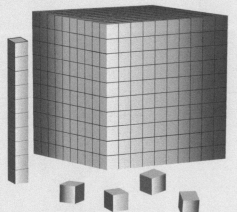

How many of the small cubes would you need to make a flat square?

How many of the flat squares would you need to make a larger cube?

How many ways can you complete this sentence?

You need a _____ to make a _____.

Place value and counting

Learn

You can partition numbers into thousands, hundreds, tens and units.

Each digit in a number represents a different value.

What do each of the digits in the number 3 333 stand for?

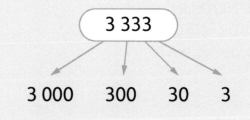

3 333

3 000   300   30   3

3 333 = 3 000 + 300 + 30 + 3

Practise

1 Express these numbers in numerals. The first one has been done for you.

a One thousand and one 1 001

b One thousand and ten

c One thousand, one hundred and ten

d Two hundred and twenty-two

e One thousand, two hundred and thirty-four

f Four thousand, three hundred and twenty-one.

2 Work out the missing numbers in these counting patterns.

a	2 000	3 000	4 000	?	?	?
b	?	?	6 000	7 000	?	?
c	1 200	1 300	1 400	?	?	?
d	?	?	2 400	2 500	?	?
e	2 100	?	4 100	?	6 100	?
f	880	890	?	?	?	?
g	2 101	?	2 103	?	2 105	?
h	2 003	2 002	2 001	?	?	?

3 Partition each number in two different ways. The first one has been done for you.

a 4 444 = 4 000 + 400 + 40 + 4 or 3 400 + 1 000 + 44

b 5 454   c 4 545   d 4 040

e 5 005   f 5 544   g 4 455

Try this

Using only the digits 1 or 2, make a four-digit number that is found between each pair of numbers.

a 1 100 and 1 200   b 2 100 and 2 200   c 1 110 and 1 120

d 2 110 and 2 120   e 2 120 and 2 200   f 2 200 and 2 300

1b Rounding and estimating

Explore

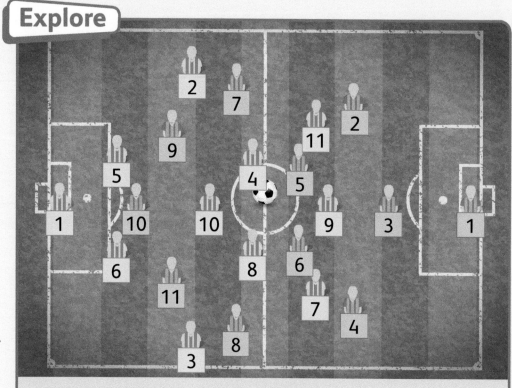

Key words
estimate
number line
hundred
thousand
to round

A football pitch is about 100 m long.

Look at the pitch. Choose three different players.
Estimate how many metres they are from each of the goals.

Placing numbers on a number line

Learn

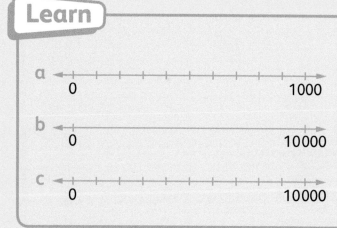

Compare these number lines.
What is the same and what is different about them?

Where would 900 go on each number line?

On which number line can you put 900 most accurately?

Practise

1 Which numbers do the arrows point to? Write the letters and the answer. The first letter has been done for you.

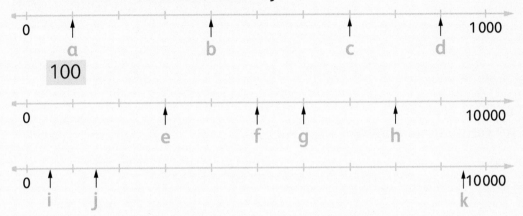

a
100

2 Show the numbers by estimating accurately on a number line.

a Draw a number line from 2 000 to 3 000. Show: 2 200, 2 400, 2 600 and 2 800.

b Draw a number line from 5 000 to 6 000. Show 5 100, 5 300, 5 500, 5 700 and 5 900.

c Draw a number line from 7 000 to 8 000. Show 7 400, 7 500 and 7 600.

d Draw a number line from 9 000 to 10 000. Show 9 999, 9 001, 9 500 and 9 050.

3 Copy these number lines. Draw an arrow to show where 5 555 would be on each number line.

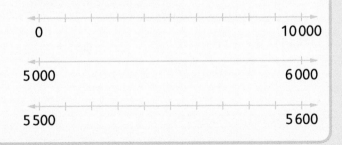

Try this

1 What is the same and what is different about these unfamiliar number lines?

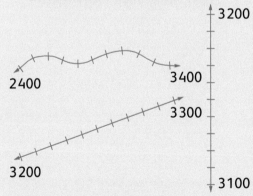

2 Draw your own creative number lines.

Rounding to the nearest 10 and 100

Learn

Where would 325 be on each number line?

320 ──────────────── 330

300 ──────────────── 400

Use this to help you round 325 to the nearest ten and to the nearest hundred.

If a number ends in 5, it rounds up to the nearest 10.

Practise

1 Round to the nearest 10. The first one has been done for you.

  a 36 40   b 236   c 436

  d 74   e 474   f 774

2 Round each number to the nearest 10, and to the nearest 100.

> 309 291 301
>   249
> 299   310
>   349

3 Write four different possible starting numbers for each of these clues.

I am thinking of a mystery number that …

  a Rounds to 100 when you round it to the nearest 10.

  b Rounds to 200 when you round it to the nearest 100, and to 150 when you round it to the nearest 10.

  c Rounds to 290 to the nearest 10, and rounds to 300 to the nearest 100.

  d Rounds to 300 when you round it to the nearest 10.

Ordering numbers

Learn

Which of these statements are incorrect? Write them correctly.

235 is less than 253

5 500 is less than 5 055

440 < 501

4 400 > 5 001

Practise

1 Write the numbers in order from smallest to largest. The first one has been done for you.

a 1 900, 1 100, 1 700, 1 300, 1 500   1 100, 1 300, 1 500, 1 700, 1 900

b 2 200, 2 800, 2 400, 3 000, 2 600, 2 000

c 9 200, 8 300, 7 400, 6 500, 5 600

d 1 900, 210, 170, 2 300, 150

e 910, 2 900, 710, 900, 5 100

f 5 100, 420, 3 300, 240, 1 500

2 Pick a number from the treasure chest to make these statements correct. Use each number once only.

? < 3 232

3 232 < ?

? > 2 323

2 332 > ?

? < 3 993

? > 3 535

3 553   2 322   3 332   3 553   3 230   3 533   2 331

Try this

▲ stands for my mystery number.

Here are some clues about my number:

It is an odd number.

It has 2 digits.

▲ > 90.

What numbers could ▲ be?

1c Addition and subtraction

Explore

This unit will teach you how to use your brain as a calculator, by using pencil and paper and your thinking skills.

What can a calculator do better than a human?

What mathematics can a human do better than a calculator?

Can you guess what any of the unusual buttons do on a calculator?

Key words

add
addition
subtract
subtraction
take away
estimate
predict

Estimate and predict

Learn

Round each number to the nearest ten.

48 rounds up to 50,
27 rounds up to 30.

50 + 30 = 80

How does this show that the calculation was wrong?

$$48 + 27 = 95$$

Practise

1 Two calculations are incorrect. Use estimation to find them. Write the letters.

a 35 + 21 = 56   b 301 + 297 = 598

c 209 + 301 = 610   d 449 + 349 = 798

e 299 + 199 = 398   f 780 + 89 = 869

2 Use rounding (to the nearest dollar) to estimate how much money was spent each week.

Price list

Bottle of juice   99c
Loaf of bread   89c
Shampoo   199c
Can of beans   49c
Bunch of bananas   79c

Week 1	
Week 2	
Week 3	

3 Look at the shopping price list again.

In week 4, approximately $5 was spent. What could have been bought?

Make two different lists that total approximately $5.

Try this

Make up two or three story problems to go with the shopping prices in question 2.

Challenge a partner to see if he or she can solve each one.

Adding and subtracting mentally

Learn

Look at these two calculations:

78 – 31

78 – 29

Which of those calculations seems hardest to do mentally? Why?

What do you notice about these two number lines?

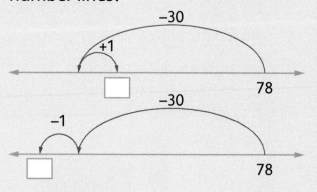

Practise

1 Add each group of numbers, by looking for pairs that total 10 or 20. The first one has been done for you.

a 12, 3, 8, 5, 7

20

12 + 3 + 8 + 5 + 7 = 20 + 10 + 5 = 35

10

b 18, 14, 2, 7, 6   c 4, 14, 6, 16, 6

d 11, 11, 9, 8, 2   e 50, 12, 15, 8, 5

2 Use mental methods to solve these calculations.

a 68 + 31
   68 + 29

b 58 – 31
   58 – 29

c 88 – 32
   88 – 28

d 51 + 42
   51 – 42

e 63 + 41
   63 – 41

f 63 + 39
   63 – 39

3 The blank boxes are where digits have gone missing.

$\boxed{}5-5\boxed{} = 38$ $\boxed{}5-5\boxed{} = 37$

How many solutions can you write?

What is the same and what is different about each solution?

Now try these:

$6\boxed{}-\boxed{}6 = 25$ $6\boxed{}-\boxed{}6 = 26$ $6\boxed{}-\boxed{}6 = 36$

Explain how the answers are related.

Adding three-digit numbers

Learn

Look at this diagram for 54 + 22:

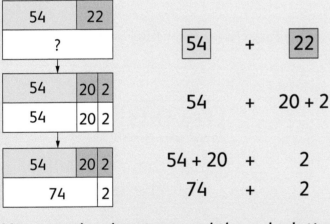

$$\boxed{54} \quad + \quad \boxed{22}$$

$$54 \quad + \quad 20 + 2$$

$$54 + 20 \quad + \quad 2$$
$$74 \quad + \quad 2$$

How are the drawings and the calculations linked?

What calculation does this diagram show?

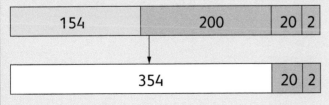

Practise

1 Write the calculations to go with these diagrams.
   The first one has been done for you.

a

234	300	40	2

234	+	300 + 40 + 2
534	+	40 + 2
574	+	2

b

243	400	30	2

c

324	300	40	2

d

422	300	30	4

e

304	400	20

f

402	30	4

2 This chart shows how much each person has saved over two weeks.
   Who has saved the most money?

Name	Week 1	Week 2
Ace	203c	332c
Zara	124c	523c
Alec	501c	130c
Lia	333c	234c
Felix	620c	38c
Irina	421c	124c

3 ☐ ☐ ☐ + ☐ ☐ ☐

Write at least five additions that have an answer less than 400.

Use the digits 1, 2, 4, 3, 0 and 0 once each.

Try this

Copy these calculations.
Write the missing digits.

$2\square4 + 42\square = 666$

$2\square5 + 53\square = 777$

$\square53 + 4\square5 = 888$

$1\square9 + 88\square = 999$

Subtracting three-digit and two-digit numbers

Learn

What is the same and what is different about these diagrams?

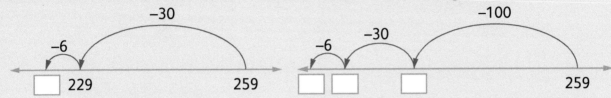

259 – 30 = 229

229 – 6 = ☐

What calculations would go with this diagram?

Practise

1 How are the answers linked in these subtractions? The first one has been done for you.

   a 258 – 26 and 258 – 126   258 – 26 = 232 (100 more than) 258 –126 = 132

   b 358 – 44 and 358 – 144   c 579 – 133 and 579 – 33

   How could you work out 876 – 232, if you know that 876 – 32 = 844?

2 Solve these subtractions:

   a 86 – 42   b 74 – 31   c 53 – 22
      186 – 42   274 – 31   353 – 22
      286 – 143   474 – 32   553 – 23

3 The children are running a race. The track is 450 m long. How much further does each person have to run? The first one has been done for you.

	Runner	Has already run	Calculation
a	Felix	220 m	450 m – 220 m = 230 m
b	Irina	321 m	
c	Alec	330 m	
d	Orlando	245 m	
e	Lia	121 m	
f	Nita	129 m	

Try this

Using the digits 5, 7 and 8 once each, write at least three solutions that have an even answer to each of these.

| | | | – 123 | | | | |–132 |

Checking strategies

Learn

There are four related addition and subtraction facts for this bar diagram.

157	
125	32

?	
125	32

$125 + 32 = 157$

157	
125	?

$157 - 125 = 32$

?	
32	125

$32 + 125 = 157$

157	
?	32

$157 - 32 = 125$

Knowing how to use these four facts can help you check your work.

What are the facts linked with $257 + 41 = 298$?

Practise

1 Draw a bar diagram to go with each calculation, and then write four facts for each. The first one has been done for you.

a $3 + 4 = 7$

7	
3	4

$4 + 3 = 7$ $7 - 4 = 3$ $7 - 3 = 4$

b $30 + 40 = 70$ c $130 + 40 = 170$

d $135 + 241 = 376$ e $9 - 4 = 5$

f $90 - 40 = 50$ g $190 - 50 = 140$

h $198 - 151 = 47$

2 Add these in a different order to check. How many of the calculations were incorrect?

   a   1 + 2 + 3 + 4 + 5 + 6 = 21

   b   3 + 4 + 5 + 4 + 3 = 25

   c   1 + 2 + 3 + 4 + 3 + 2 + 1 = 16

   d   10 + 20 + 30 + 20 + 1 = 100

   e   7 + 10 + 5 + 15 + 30 = 57

   f   14 + 20 + 41 + 6 + 11 = 92

I find a number line helps.

3 Use reasoning on a number line.

Draw a number line to solve each addition.
Then, draw a second number line to show the inverse operation. The first one has been done for you.

   a   155 + 30 = **185**

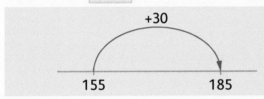

          +30   −30

     155   185   155   185

   b   266 + 33 = ☐   c   377 + 130 = ☐   d   377 + 133 = ☐

   e   488 + 30 = ☐   f   488 + 233 = ☐

Try this

I use different methods depending on the numbers.

1 Show two different strategies to solve each calculation. Explain which method you prefer and why.

  555 + 44

  12 + 87

  999 − 88

2 Write four different story problems for the four number facts that go with 99 + 50.

Self-check

A Place value and decimals

1 Write ten more than each of these numbers.
   a 2 222   b 3 333   c 4 444

2 Write 100 more than each of these numbers.
   a 4 321   b 5 432   c 6 543

B Rounding and estimating

1 Write these numbers in order from smallest to biggest.

2 Round each number to the nearest 10.

3 Draw a number line to show the numbers accurately.

C Addition and subtraction

1 Estimate which of these calculations will give an answer bigger than 100:
   a 57 + 61   b 122 – 38
   c 19 + 29 + 59

2 Solve these additions and subtractions:
   a 54 + 21   b 54 – 21
   c 154 + 19   d 154 – 19

3 Solve these additions and subtractions:
   a 234 + 415   b 523 – 211

4 Write four facts using the numbers 250, 120 and 370.

Unit 2 Measures and problem solving

2a The metric system

Explore

height

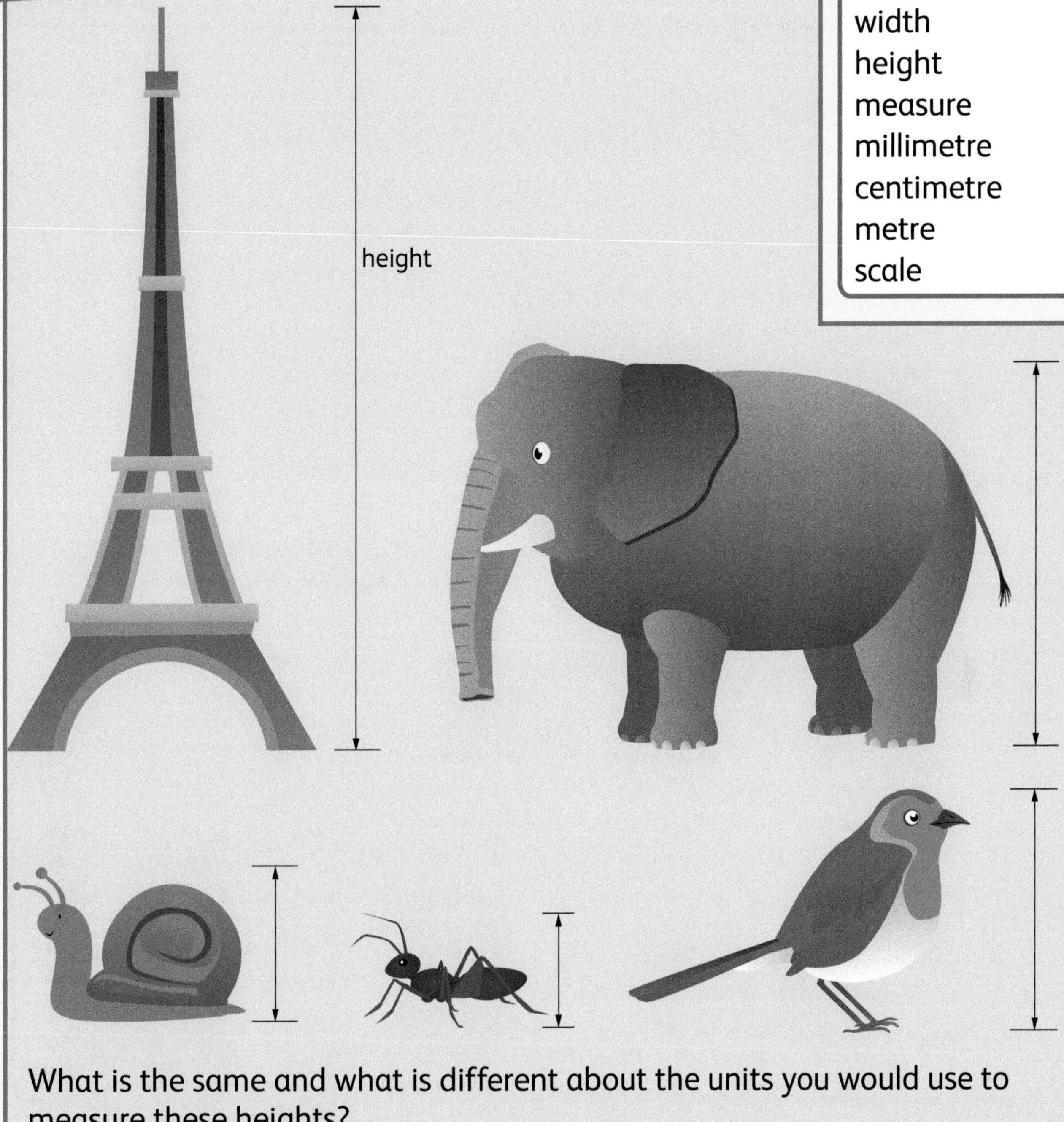

What is the same and what is different about the units you would use to measure these heights?

List the different units for measuring length that you know.

Measuring length, width and height

Learn

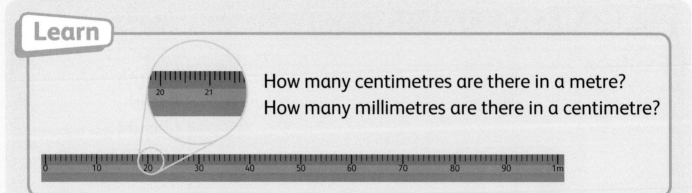

How many centimetres are there in a metre?
How many millimetres are there in a centimetre?

Practise

1 Measure each of these lines. Write the measurement in cm or in mm.

2 a Estimate the number of millimetres shown.

b Estimate the number of centimetres shown.

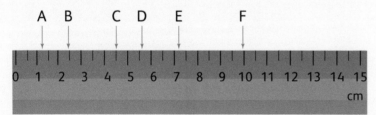

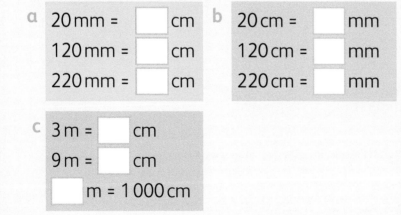

3 Convert these measures.

a 20 mm = ☐ cm   b 20 cm = ☐ mm

120 mm = ☐ cm   120 cm = ☐ mm

220 mm = ☐ cm   220 cm = ☐ mm

c 3 m = ☐ cm

9 m = ☐ cm

☐ m = 1 000 cm

Try this

Look around your classroom to find an object as close in length as possible to:

2 m   110 cm   10 mm

90 mm   900 mm

1 000 mm   900 cm

2b Length, area and perimeter

Explore

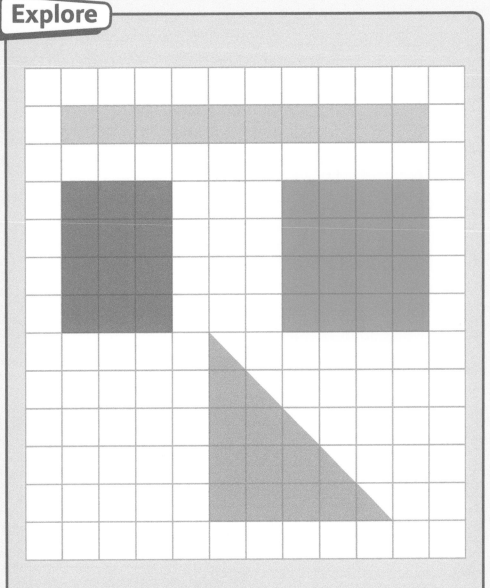

Key words
length
perimeter
area
centimetre
measure

Which shape is the biggest?

Could 'biggest' mean different things?

Biggest could mean the tallest, longest or widest shape. It could mean the shape that covers the largest number of squares. In mathematics, we need to use more specific words.

Working out perimeter

Learn

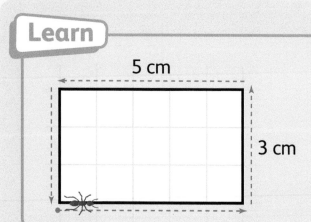

Perimeter is the distance in a line all the way around the outline of a shape.

Perimeter is given in units of distance, for example centimetres or metres, just like when you measure a straight line.

How far does this ant have to walk?

5 cm + 3 cm + 5 cm + 3 cm = 16 cm

Practise

1 Calculate how far each ant has to walk. Show your calculations for each rectangle. The first one has been done for you.

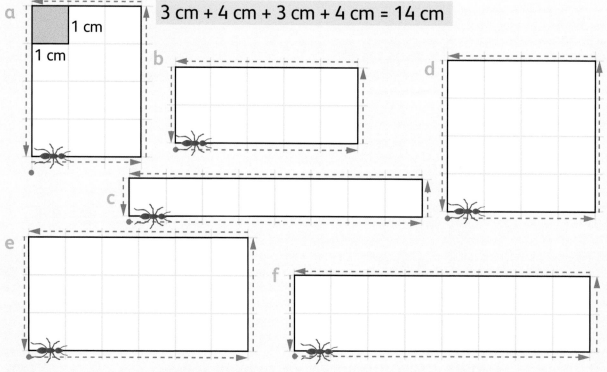

a   3 cm + 4 cm + 3 cm + 4 cm = 14 cm

Which ant has to walk the furthest?

2 Use a ruler to draw rectangles with these measurements.

a 5 cm wide and 3 cm tall   b 6 cm wide and 4 cm tall

c 7 cm wide and 2 cm tall   d 2 cm wide and 9 cm tall

e 10 cm wide and 1 cm tall   f 3 cm wide and 3 cm tall.

3 Draw two different rectangles each with a perimeter of:

a 10 cm   b 20 cm

c 30 cm   d 40 cm.

Try this

Without drawing, what could be the width and length of a rectangle that had a perimeter of 100 cm?

Finding the area of a shape

Learn

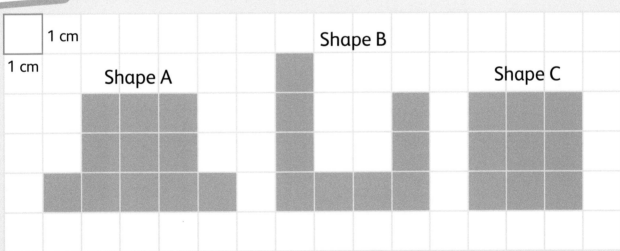

Area measures how much space a shape covers up. You can count the squares on a grid to help work it out.

Which of these shapes covers the most squares?

Shape A covers 11 squares, that is more than Shape B or C, so Shape A has the largest area.

Think like a mathematician

To be accurate, if your grid is centimetre squares, you can use the units 'centimetres squared' for area. This is usually written as cm².

Practise

1 Predict which shape has the largest area, and then check.

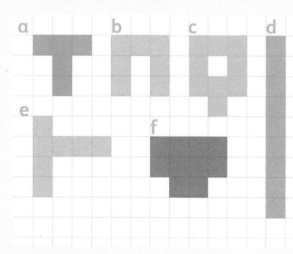

Remember to write the units as 'squares'.

2 On squared paper, draw eight different shapes. Make each with an area of ten squares.

3 Use a ruler to draw these rectangles. Then, work out how many squares each one covers.

  a Width = 5 cm, length = 5 cm

  b Width = 4 cm, length = 3 cm

  c Width = 4 cm, length = 6 cm

  d Width = 10 cm, length = 4 cm

  e Width = 8 cm, length = 3 cm

  f Width = 2 cm, length = 12 cm

Try this

This rectangle has a perimeter of 120 cm. What could its length and width be?

Try to find three different solutions.

2c Time

Explore

Key words

time
a.m.
p.m.
midday
analogue clock
digital clock

What could each of these people do to estimate the time?

a.m. and p.m.

Learn

a.m.   p.m.

When you see a.m. it means 'before midday', and when you see p.m., it means 'after midday'.

What is the same and what is different about these times?
Would the time look similar on a digital clock?

A digital clock would show the hours and the minutes past the hour in numerals.
3 o'clock would look like this on a digital clock.

hours minutes

Quarter past 12 would look like this on a digital clock.

hours minutes

Remember that a quarter of an hour is 15 minutes. There are 60 minutes in an hour, not 100!

Practise

1 Put these times in order, from earliest to latest. The first one has been done for you.

a 7.30 p.m., 8.20 a.m., 7.20 a.m., 8.15 p.m., 7.25 p.m.

  7.20 a.m., 8.20 a.m., 7.25 p.m., 7.30 p.m., 8.15 p.m.

b 2 p.m., 2.12 a.m., 2.13 p.m., 2.15 p.m., 2 a.m., 2.01 p.m.

c 5.05 p.m., 5.50 a.m., 5.15 a.m., 5.15 p.m., 5.50 p.m., 5.05 a.m.

d Midday, 1 p.m., 3 a.m., 2 p.m., 6 a.m., 5 p.m.

2 Give each time digitally. The first one has been done for you.

a   00.30 and 18.00

3 What unit of time would you use for these events?

	Action	Unit of time	Estimate
a	Walking to school		
b	Watching a movie		
c	The length of a holiday		
d	A lesson at school		
e	Singing a nursery rhyme		
f	An advert on TV		
g	Reading a sentence from a book.		

Try this

Alec's watch is always 10 minutes fast.
Lia's watch is always slow.

Look at the pictures of their watches,
and work out how slow Lia's watch is.

Alec's watch   Lia's watch

⏻ 2d Problem solving

Explore

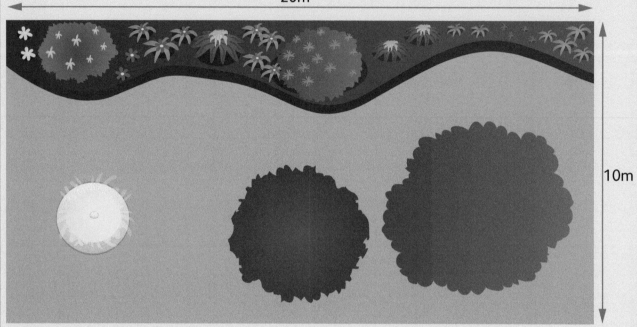

20m

10m

This garden needs a new fence to go around the edge.

Alec thinks it needs a 30 m fence.
Lia thinks it needs a 100 m fence.

Are their predictions accurate?
Explain your thinking.

Try this

Draw a diagram of your school playground. Estimate the measurements and add them to your diagram. When you get a chance, try walking around the perimeter of your playground, and see if you were right. One large stride is approximately one metre.

Key words ⏻

estimate
method
jottings
explain
reasoning
check

Problem solving using diagrams and checking your working

Practise

1 Sketch a diagram of a garden that is 10 m by 15 m.

10 m

15 m

a Add the measurements.

b Work out the perimeter of the garden.

c Show your calculations and how they match your diagram.

2 Lia's garden is 20 m by 12 m.

a Draw a diagram of the garden.

b Calculate exactly how much fence she needs.

c Make sure your calculations are shown on your diagram. Check them by adding in a different order.

3 Alec has 60 m of wire fence.

It takes Alec 5 minutes to put up 10 m of wire fence.

a Make up two story problems about Alec and his fence. One of your problems has to use the calculation $60 \div 10$.

b Swap your problem with a friend. Explain to each other how you would solve the problems. Write out your solutions to your friend's problems for him or her to check.

4 Find two rectangles in your classroom. Work with a friend to put your four rectangles (without measuring) in order from the one with the smallest perimeter to the one with the greatest. Check your order by measuring the perimeters.

Self-check

A The metric system

1 How many millimetres in five centimetres?

2 How many centimetres in five metres?

3 Which is longer: 45 mm or 6 cm?

4 How much longer is 2 m than 175 cm?

B Length, area and perimeter

1 What units are used to measure perimeter?

2 What is the perimeter of these squares?

 a 3 cm wide

 b 5 cm wide

 c 6 cm wide.

3 Draw a rectangle with an area of 6 squares.

4 Alec's rectangular garden needs 60 m of fence.

 a Draw three different diagrams to show the possible lengths and widths of his garden.

 b It takes Alec 5 minutes to put up 10 m of wire fence. How long will it take him to complete the fence?

C Time

1 Give each time digitally:

 a half past two in the afternoon

 b quarter past three a.m.

 c twenty past four p.m.

 d twenty to five in the morning.

2 Write these times in words:

 a 3.30   b 15.15

 c 9.20   d 10.10

Unit 3 Number and problem solving

3a Number patterns

Explore

 I think there are 100 fingers and thumbs here.

 I think there are 501 fingers and thumbs here.

Who do you think is closest to being right?
Are there reasons to doubt their ideas?
What different methods could you use to check?

Key words
multiple
digit
method
times table

Multiples of 5, 10 and 100

Learn

Look at the place value charts.

This place value chart shows a multiple of a hundred.

Hs	Ts	1s
5	0	0

These place value charts show a multiple of a hundred and a multiple of ten.

Hs	Ts	1s
5	5	5

Hs	Ts	1s
5	5	0

Write all the numbers.

How many multiples of five are there?

How could you convince someone that you are right?

Which is the odd one out from this list?

20, 700, 45, 90

Explain your thinking.

A multiple is a number that contains a smaller number an exact number of times, for example: 25 is a multiple of 5. 30 is a multiple of 10.

Practise

1 Choose an odd one out from each set of numbers, based on whether it is a multiple of 5, 10 or 100. The first one has been done for you.

a 800, 400, 200, 650, 900, 100

650 is the odd one out as it is not a multiple of 100.

b 30, 130, 230, 530, 635, 730   c 30, 430, 500, 670, 910, 90

d 20, 120, 95, 220, 810, 440   e 940, 930, 920, 910, 900, 890

f 125, 555, 520, 800, 225, 995

2 Complete the following number challenges.
  Use each multiple of 5 once only.

  a ? + ? = a multiple of 5

  b ? + ? = a multiple of 100

  c ? + ? + ? = a multiple of 10

  25   110   60   120   90   250   10

3 Now do the same using these multiples of 5.

  225 230 240 270 290 300 310

4 Decide if each statement is always true.

  a Adding two multiples of 5 makes a multiple of 10.

  b Adding two multiples of 5 gives a multiple of 5.

  c If you subtract a multiple of 10 from a multiple of 100, you get a multiple
    of 10.

  d If you add three multiples of 5, you do not get a multiple of 10.

  If you think a statement is not always true, write an example that shows
  it can be wrong.

Try this

These statements are *sometimes* true:
● The sum of two multiples of 5 ends in a 5.
● The sum of three multiples of 5 ends in a 5.
● The sum of four multiples of 5 ends in a 0.

Find three examples that are true for each statement.
Find another three examples that are false for each statement.

Recognising multiples of 2, 3 and 4

Learn

Where would these numbers go in the Venn diagram?

| 4 | 12 | 9 | 18 | 3 | 21 |

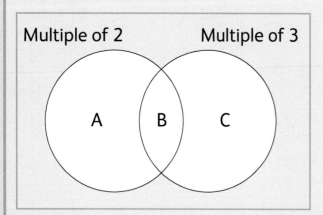

Multiple of 2   Multiple of 3

A   B   C

Think of numbers that would not go in A, B or C.

Practise

1 a Write down three numbers to go in each section of the diagram. What do you notice about the numbers that go in section B?

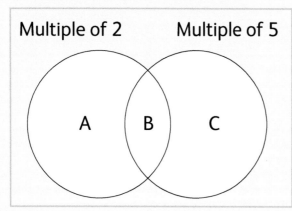

Multiple of 2   Multiple of 5

A   B   C

b Now look at this Venn diagram. Try to find three numbers to go in each section. What do you notice?

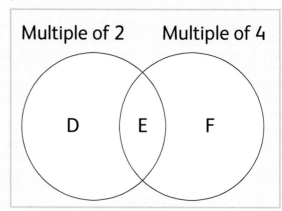

Multiple of 2   Multiple of 4

D   E   F

2 Look at the patterns of multiples in the clouds below.

   a Continue each pattern of multiples, but do not go past the number 50.

Multiples of 3
0, 3, 6, 9, 12, …

Multiples of 4
0, 4, 8, 12, 16, …

   b What is the largest number in your lists that is a multiple of both 3 and 4?

   c Are there any numbers in each list that are also multiples of 5?

3 Decide if each statement is always, sometimes, or never true. Explain your reasoning for each answer.

b Multiples of 4 are odd.

c Multiples of 4 end in a 4 or an 8.

a Multiples of 3 are odd.

d Multiples of 4 are also multiples of 2.

Find examples for each statement to explain your reasoning.

Try this

Think of a way of finding a multiple of 3 or 4 that has three digits.
See if you can find at least three different multiples of 3 and 4 that have three digits.

 ## 3b **Multiplication and division**

 Weighs 3 kg

These boxes are stored in patterns like this.
What would the next few stacks look like?

Think of two different calculations to work out the weight of each stack.

Key words
multiply
times
groups
array
divide
division
share
inverse

Multiply a pair of digits

Learn

What is the same and what is different about these two arrays?
What different calculations do they represent?

___ × ___

___ + ___ + ___ + ___

___ × ___

___ + ___ + ___ + ___ + ___

Which do you find easiest to calculate?

Practise

1 Write two different multiplications to go with each array. The first one has been done for you.

a **3 × 4 OR 4 × 3**   b   c

2 Draw an array to represent these repeated additions.

Then write a multiplication calculation to go with each one. The first one has been done for you.

a 5 + 5

b 6 + 6 + 6

c 2 + 2 + 2 + 2

d 3 + 3 + 3 + 3 + 3 + 3

e 4 + 4

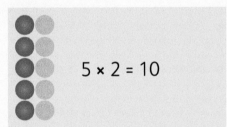

5 × 2 = 10

3 Look at the stacks of boxes below and write the calculations. Calculate how much Stack A, B and C would weigh. The first one has been done for you.

The boxes each have a mass of:

a 3 kg   Stack A weighs 3 + 3 + 3 = 9 kg or 3 × 3 = 9 kg.

b 6 kg   c 7 kg   d 10 kg   e 9 kg

Stack C

Stack B

Stack A

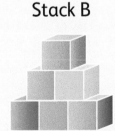

Multiplying by 10

Learn

These place-value charts show how digits change when a number is multiplied by 10. Write a calculation for each diagram.

Hs	Ts	1s
	3	5
3	5	0

Hs	Ts	1s
	5	3
5	3	0

This picture shows the effect of multiplying by 10.

$\square$ × 10 =

Copy and complete the missing numbers in the chart below.

33 × 10 = ☐

Hs	Ts	1s
	3	3

550 ÷ 10 = ☐

Hs	Ts	1s
5	5	0

Practise

1 Copy and complete. The first one has been done for you.

a 13 × 10 = 130
   23 × 10 = ☐
   230 × 10 = ☐
   235 × 10 = ☐

b ☐ × 10 = 190
   ☐ × 10 = 380
   ☐ × 10 = 3 800
   ☐ × 10 = 3 840

c 450 ÷ 10 = ☐
   540 ÷ 10 = ☐
   ☐ ÷ 10 = 36
   ☐ ÷ 10 = 63

2 Use these digit cards more than once each to make multiplications and divisions. How many solutions can you find? The first one has been done for you.

2 5 0 ×10 ÷10 =

2 5 ×10 = 2 5 0

Try this

Use your multiplying and dividing skills to draw these diagrams.

a A rectangle with a perimeter of 160 mm
b A rectangle with a perimeter of 260 mm
c A square with a perimeter of 200 mm.

Multiplying by 10, 20, 30 …

Learn

I know 5 × 3 = 15, but what is 50 × 3?
Look at these diagrams for help.

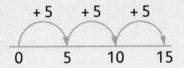

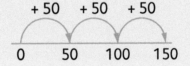

Practise

1 Copy and complete these multiplications. The first one has been done for you.

a
10 × 3 = 30
20 × 3 = ☐
50 × 3 = ☐
90 × 3 = ☐

b
10 × 5 = ☐
20 × 5 = ☐
50 × 5 = ☐
90 × 5 = ☐

2 What calculations would help you work out these?

a How many seconds are there in five minutes?

b How many minutes are there in five hours?

c How many days are there in 20 weeks?

Try this

I am thinking of a mystery number. I multiply it by 10.

I am thinking of a number. I double it.

Alec and Lia both end up with the same answer.

What could their starting numbers have been?
Write at least five solutions.

Multiplying two-digit numbers

Learn

How could you solve 3 × 13?

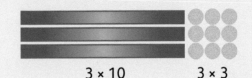

3 × 13   3 × 10   3 × 3

Now you can work out 13 × 3:

3 × 10 = 30

3 × 3 = 9

13 × 3 = 30 + 9.

What would you do for 3 × 23?

Practise

1 Draw an array, or use tens and ones blocks, to solve these multiplications. The first one has been done for you.

a 3 × 12  3 × 10 + 3 × 2

b 5 × 13

c 7 × 14

d 6 × 15

2 What multiplications do these diagrams show?

Solve each calculation.

3 a How many hours are there in three days?

b How many hours are there in a week?

c How many hours are there in eight days?

There are 24 hours in one day.

43

Multiplication and division

Learn

Look at this multiplication triangle:

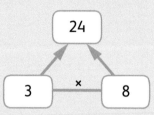

You can find out four facts from this diagram:

◻ × ◻ = 24   24 ÷ ◻ = ◻

◻ × ◻ = 24   24 ÷ ◻ = ◻

Try this

◻◻ × ◻

What is the multiplication you can write with the largest answer using each card once?

What is the product with the the smallest answer you can write?

Practise

1 Write four facts to go with each of the diagrams below. The first one has been done for you.

a
18

6   ×   3

b
18

9   ×   2

c
36

9   ×   4

6 × 3 = 18   18 ÷ 6 = 3
3 × 6 = 18   18 ÷ 3 = 6

2 Copy and complete these diagrams.

a
15

3   ×   ◻

b
20

5   ×   ◻

c
28

4   ×   ◻

d
36

◻   ×   3

15 ÷ 3 = ◻   20 ÷ 5 = ◻   28 ÷ 4 = ◻   36 ÷ 3 = ◻

3 Pens come in packs of 4, but pencils come in packs of 6. How many packs should I buy? The first one has been done for you.
I need:

a 32 pens

> Pens come in packs of 4. 32 ÷ 4 = 8.
> I need 8 packs of pens.

b 24 pencils

c 44 pens

d 36 pencils

e 80 pens

f 120 pencils.

Try this

> 64 ÷ 4 = 14
> But 14 × 4 = 56

I knew I got this division wrong because I checked by multiplying.

Do a multiplication to check if each division is correct:

51 ÷ 3 = 18

52 ÷ 4 = 13

60 ÷ 4 = 16

96 ÷ 6 = 16

128 ÷ 8 = 16

Dividing a two-digit number

Learn

What is 51 ÷ 3?

10 × 3 = 30 is too low, 20 × 3 = 60 is too high.
The answer has to be between 10 and 20.

You could just start at 10 × 3, and add on 3 at a time:

10 × 3 = 30, 11 × 3 = 33 … still too low
12 × 3 = 36 … still too low
Keep going until you reach 51.

Is there a faster way?

This bar diagram shows a way to work out 51 ÷ 3.

10 × 3 = 30, and 7 × 3 = 21.
How many lots of 3 make 51?

? × 3 = 51

51	
30	21

10 × 3   ☐ × 3

Try this

Alec and Lia have been saving up.

Lia saves $5 a week. Alec saves $6 a week.

Lia wants to buy a bicycle that costs $65.

Alec wants to buy roller skates that cost $72.

Who will reach their target first?

Practise

1 Copy and complete these diagrams to work out each division:

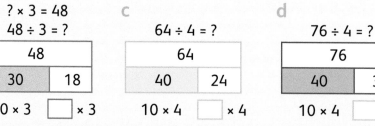

a   ? × 3 = 54
   54 ÷ 3 = ?

54	
30	24

10 × 3 ☐ × 3

b   ? × 3 = 48
   48 ÷ 3 = ?

48	
30	18

10 × 3 ☐ × 3

c   64 ÷ 4 = ?

64	
40	24

10 × 4 ☐ × 4

d   76 ÷ 4 = ?

76	
40	36

10 × 4 ☐ × 4

2 Draw a bar model to show each multiplication. Then write the division fact:

a 22 × 4 = ?   b 25 × 3 = ?

3 Use the multiplication facts to help you to work out:

a ☐ ÷ 4 = 23   b 78 ÷ 3 = ☐

3c Problem solving

What could you do to estimate how many people there are in the audience?

Key words
estimate
predict
check
explain

Estimating and predicting

Learn

What is the difference between estimating and predicting?

Predicting is like a guess, but you think of reasons before you guess. Estimating is when you think of reasons for an answer that might be close, but may not be exact.

Practise

1 300 people want to watch the new film.

In a cinema, there are:

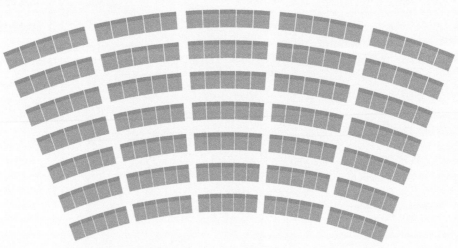

Just by looking, can you estimate if there are enough seats? Then check using an appropriate calculation.

How many people will miss out?

2

> I am going to read 5 pages today. I think that will be more than 500 words.

> On my page there are 120 words, and 6 words on a line.

Does Lia's prediction seem reasonable?

There are eight words on each line, and 25 lines per page.

How many words are there on a page?

Was she right?

How many lines are there on a page in Alec's book?

3 Bamboo is one of the fastest-growing plants in the world. It can grow 1 mm in a minute and a half.

Lia thinks the plant will grow 60 mm in an hour.

Explain why she must be wrong.

How much would it grow in three minutes?

How much would it grow in six minutes?

How long until it reached 20 cm long?

4 Write a different story problem for each of these calculations:

a 3 × 4

b 4 × 3

c 9 × 5

d 5 × 9

Compare your problems with your partner, and see if you agree that he or she matches the calculations.

Try this

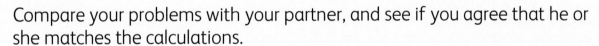

Take a reading book. Make an estimate of the number of words per page. Do this by counting how many words there are on most lines, and how many lines there are on a page.

How many pages would you have to read before you reached 1 000 words?

Self-check

A Number patterns

1 Copy the table below. Write five different numbers for each heading.

Multiple of 2	
Multiple of 3	
Multiple of 4	
Multiple of 5	
Multiple of 10	
Multiple of 100	

B Multiplication and division

1 Draw an array to work out 5×8.

2 Write the answers to these calculations.

   a $56 \times 10 = \boxed{}$ b $\boxed{} \times 10 = 650$

3 Write the answers to these:

   a 20×3 b 30×3 c 40×3

4 Which is bigger: 24×5 or 25×4?

5 Write the answers to these:

   a $21 \div 3 = \boxed{}$ b $81 \div 3 = \boxed{}$ c $99 \div 3 = \boxed{}$

4a Classifying shapes

Explore

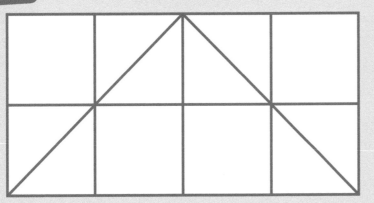

How many different shapes are hidden in this diagram?

Can you see different hexagons or pentagons?

What is the shape with the largest number of corners?

Key words

classify

2-D

polygon

quadrilateral

triangle

hexagon

pentagon

right angle

Drawing and reasoning about polygons

Learn

This is a nine-dot grid and a nine-pin geoboard.

Use dotty paper, or make a dotty grid on paper. You could also use a pinboard.

How many different triangles can you design? Aim to find at least five different triangles

You can use them for designing different 2-D shapes.

These shapes are called polygons. Polygons are 2-D shapes made from straight lines.

Think of specific names for each of the polygons shown.

Practise

1 Use a nine-dot grid or pinboard and make these shapes.

   a A triangle

   b A rectangle

   c A square

   d A four-sided shape
      that is not a rectangle

   e A four-sided shape with exactly two right angles.

> A right angle is a quarter-turn. You often see them in the corner of a book, or any square or rectangle.

2 Look at these shapes on a 3-by-3 grid:

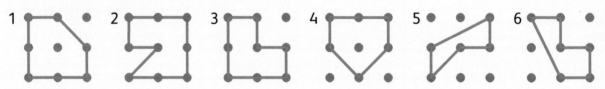

   a Which shapes are hexagons?

   b Which shape is a hexagon with three right angles?

   c Which shape is a pentagon with one right angle?

   d Which hexagon has the most right angles?

   e Are there any shapes with an even number of right angles?

Think like a mathematician

Remember – a right angle does not always go vertically or horizontally. They can also be 'tilted'.

4b 3-D and 2-D shapes

Explore

These are nets. They fold to make 3-D shapes. Agree with a partner what you can work out about the 3-D shapes these nets would make.

How many vertices, edges or faces would each shape have?

Lines of symmetry

Learn

Predict how many corners these shapes will have once they are completed across their mirror lines.

Name the shapes.

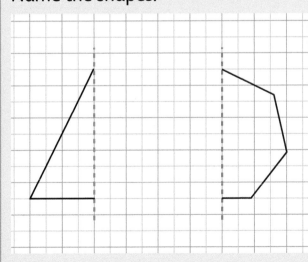

Draw a straight line across an object to divide it into two pieces. If the one side is a mirror image of the other side, then the object is symmetrical.

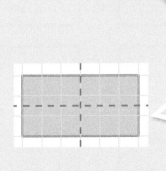

Practise

1 Look at these shapes. Predict how many corners each will have when it is complete. The first one has been done for you.

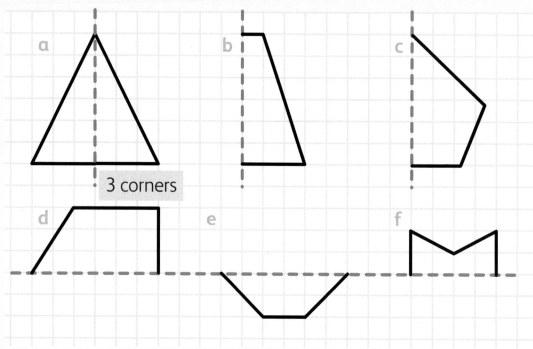

3 corners

2 What is the smallest number of squares you need to add to make each shape symmetrical across its mirror line?

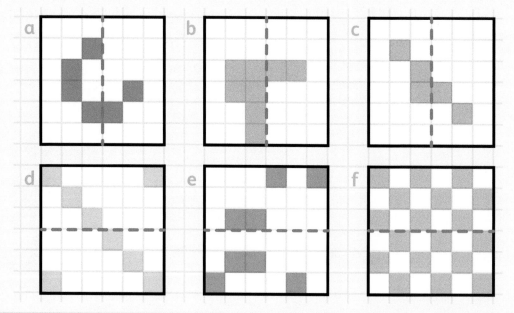

4c **Position and movement**

Explore

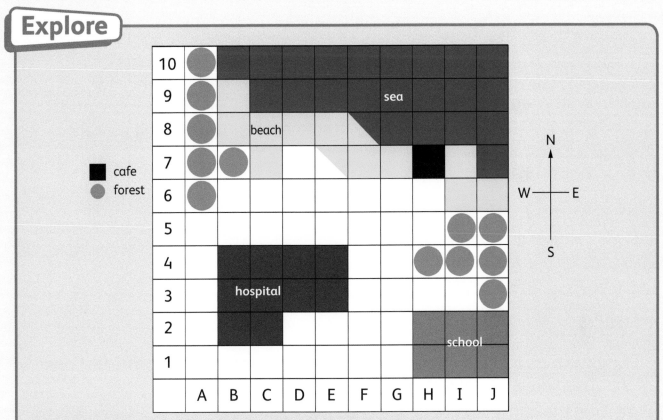

Describe the position of the school on the map.

What do you think the letters and numbers are used for?

Why would you have to be careful at H9?

You are at the cafe, facing north. You turn a right angle anti-clockwise. Which way are you facing now?

You are at the school facing west. What turn do you have to make to face the cafe?

Think like a mathematician

Square grids can be used to identify locations because every square has its own unique letter and number, called a grid reference. The horizontal label is always given before the vertical one.

Key words

turn
right angle
90 degrees
grid reference
direction

Grid references

Learn

5					
4		●		●	
3					
2		●			
1					
	A	B	C	D	E

The dots mark the corners of a square. The grid reference for one corner is B4. What is the grid reference of the missing corner?

Practise

1 Use the map in the 'Explore' panel to answer these questions. The first one has been done for you.

 a Give the grid reference for the cafe. H7

 b Give the grid reference for each part of the hospital.

 c Give the grid reference for each part of the school.

 d Which of these grid references are not in the sea? H10, A10, D10, B1, E9

2 Look at the two grids below. The dots mark the corners of squares. There are two squares hidden in each grid.

 Give the grid reference for the corners of both squares in each grid.

a
5	●				●
4			●		
3		●		●	
2			●		
1	●				●
	A	B	C	D	E

b
5	●			●	
4			●		●
3					
2	●		●	●	●
1					
	A	B	C	D	E

4d Problem solving

Explore

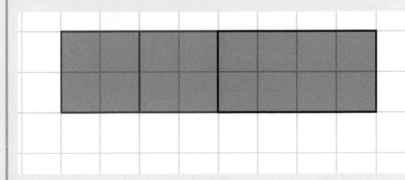

A   B   C

Follow these instructions to make a square from a rectangle of paper.

Key words
quadrilateral
triangle
polygon
right angle
diagonal
composite shape

Composite shapes

Learn

A composite shape is made by joining two or more shapes together.

Look at this shape.

It is made from a rectangle and two squares.

A shape with four straight sides and four corners is called a quadrilateral.

Could you rearrange them to make a square?

How can you be sure?

Practise

1 Use the three shapes in the 'Learn' panel to make five different shapes.

   Draw a diagram and write the name of each shape. One has been done for you.

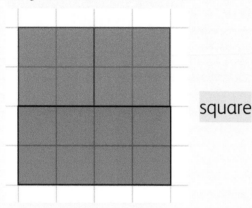

square

2 Make two identical squares, as in the 'Explore' panel.

   a Cut each square in half, diagonally. Now you should have four identical triangles.

   b Use two of the triangles to make:
   ● a triangle
   ● a four-sided shape that is not a square.

   c Use all four triangles to make:
   ● a rectangle
   ● a triangle
   ● a square
   ● a different quadrilateral.

   d What shapes can you make using only three triangles? The sides have to match up.

   e Can you make a rectangle with nine triangles? What about ten?

   Explain why you need a certain number of triangles to make a rectangle.

   Now investigate how many triangles you need to make a square.

Try this

Make a square out of paper. Fold it in half along four different lines.

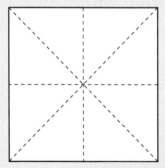

Cut out all eight triangles.

See how many different shapes you can make using the 8 triangles and matching up sides.

Can you make a shape with 3 sides, with 4 sides, with 5 sides, or more?

Reasoning about quadrilaterals

Learn

There are many different types of quadrilaterals.

Is this rectangle a quadrilateral?

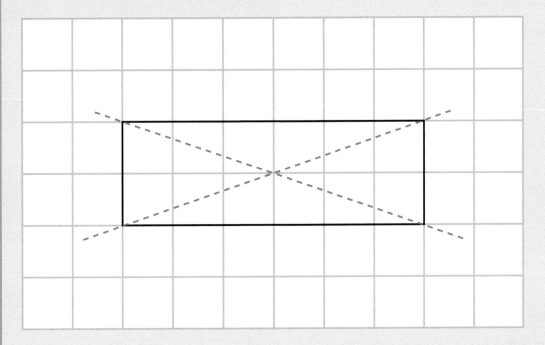

The diagonals of this rectangle have been drawn, by joining opposite corners.

The diagonals of this rectangle cross at right angles. True or false?

How can you tell?

Try this

Follow the instructions to make a square in the 'Explore' panel on page 57. Then fold your square in half, and in half again. When you open it, you will have four right angles of 90 degrees each around the centre. You can use this square to test if other objects in your classroom also have right angles.

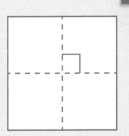

Practise

1 a Draw five different squares and then mark the diagonals by joining opposite corners.

   The diagonals of a square cross at right angles. True or false?

  b Now, draw five different rectangles.

   The diagonals of a rectangle cross at right angles. True or false?

2 Here are the definitions of some different quadrilaterals.

A **rhombus** has four sides that are the same length.

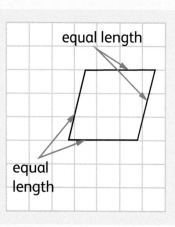

In a **kite**, opposite sides are different lengths, but joined pairs of sides are the same length.

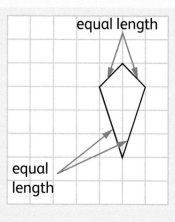

  a Draw five different kites, and five different rhombuses.

  b A rhombus always has two lines of symmetry. True or false?

  c A kite never has lines of symmetry. True or false?

3 Which of these shapes has an odd number of vertices? Do any have an odd number of edges? Explain what you find out.

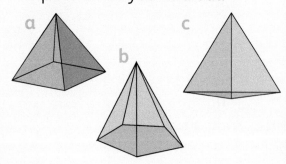

Try this

Draw two lines that cross at right angles and halve each other. Join the ends of the lines together to make a quadrilateral.

List all the different shapes you can make in this way.

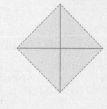

Try this

Which of these pictures of the environment and art have shapes in them?
Which are symmetrical?
Collect pictures from newspapers and magazines (or from the internet if you have access) that have symmetrical objects or shapes in them.
Identify the shapes. Tell your partner why you think they have symmetry.

Self-check

A **Classifying shapes**

   1   Draw three different four-sided shapes.

   2   What is the name for a shape that has six corners?

   3   How many corners are there on an octagon?

B **3-D and 2-D shapes**

   1   Draw a symmetrical triangle and a triangle that has no lines of symmetry.

   2   Name an object in your classroom that is symmetrical.

   3   Draw a pentagon with a line of symmetry.

C **Position and movement**

   1   Look at the 'Explore' panel on page 55. Write the grid references for the four trees that are nearest to the school.

   2   Look at the 'Learn panel' on page 56. What kind of triangle do the dots make?

Unit 5   Problem solving and review

5a Problem solving

Explore

Price list

Adults $5
Children $3

Opening times:
11 a.m. to 9 p.m.

COCONUT SHY

Think like a mathematician

Look carefully for information in the picture. It will help you to solve the story problems on the next few pages.

Key words

puzzle
solution
problem
solve
predict
estimate
calculate

Story problems

1 How long will the people have to wait until the fairground opens?

2 How much will the queuing people spend on tickets in total?

3 Some children arrive at 6:30 p.m. How many minutes will they have until the fairground closes?

4 A group of adults and children arrived. There were ten people altogether. They spent a total of $44. How many adults and how many children were there in the group?

5 Write your own word problem about how much it costs to go to the fairground with a group, or about how long they will have at the fairground. Be ready to share your problems with the class.

Try this

For how many hours is the fairground open every day?

For how many hours is it open for a whole week?

How much more would a child spend than an adult if he or she visited every day from Monday to Friday?

Calculation problems

1 Each compartment can carry ten people. How many people can ride at once?

2 Half of the compartments are empty and half are full.

How many spaces are empty?

3 Another Ferris wheel has 30 compartments. The total number of people the two wheels can carry is the same. How many people can fit in each compartment of this second Ferris wheel?

4 It takes the wheel one and a half minutes to turn around once. In a ride, the wheel turns six times. How long does the ride last in total?

5 Design three different Ferris wheels that can carry exactly 60 people at once.

6 Now design three different Ferris wheels that can carry exactly 120 people at once.

Try this

The world's first Ferris wheel was in Chicago, USA in 1893. It could carry 60 people in a single compartment!

a How long ago was it invented?

b How many people could it carry in ten compartments?

c How many people could it carry in five compartments?

d How many people could it carry in 20 compartments?

e In total there were 36 compartments. Try to use your answers to work out how many people could travel at one time.

Think like a mathematician

If you know how many people travel in ten compartments, then you can double that number, or halve the number to work out 20 compartments or five compartments. That will give you all the numbers you need to work out how many people there are in 35 compartments.

Pattern problems

1 The fairground owner wants the carts to be joined together in a line so that no carts of the same colour are next to each other.

Design five different ways of arranging the carts.

2 One of the yellow carts and one of the blue carts are damaged.
Find six different solutions using only the four remaining carts.

3 Another roller coaster owner wants to split the six carts into two groups of three. In how many different ways can this be done? Write all the possible solutions.

Here is one solution to get you started:

4 On a different roller coaster, there is a red, a green, a blue and a yellow cart. Can these carts be arranged in more than ten different ways?

Puzzle problems

This is the time on Alec's watch when he arrived at the fairground.

He spent double the amount of time on the roller coaster than he did on the Ferris wheel. He spent half an hour less on the coconut shy than he did on the roller coaster. He spent 15 minutes on the Ferris wheel.

What time did he finish?

6a   Numbers and the number system

Explore

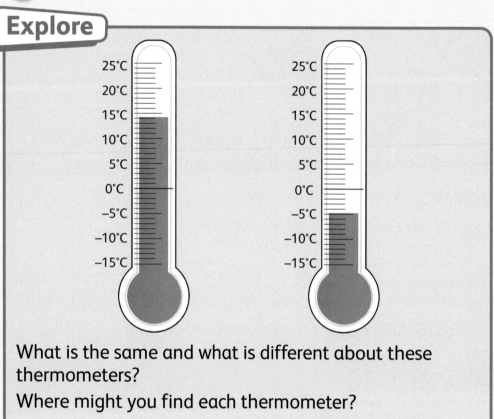

What is the same and what is different about these thermometers?

Where might you find each thermometer?

Key words

thousand

partition

negative

round

decimal

Partitioning numbers

Learn

Which of these calculations makes the largest number?

1000 + 100 + 10 + 1?

1000 + 210 + 20 + 4

4000 + 300 + 20 + 1?

4000 + 200 + 110 + 1

1 + 30 + 500 + 7000?

4000 + 100 + 211 + 11

Think of two different calculations to make 9876.

1 Partition these numbers in two different ways.
The first one has been done for you.

a 5100   5 000 + 100 or 3 000 + 2 100   b 5010

c 5001   d 1005   e 1050   f 1500

Using place value to add and subtract numbers close to 100

Learn

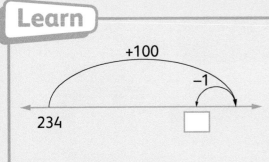

234 +100 −1 ☐

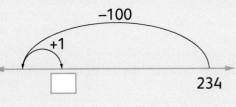

−100 +1 ☐ 234

I can add 99 by adding 100, so the hundreds digit increases by one, then subtracting one, so the ones digit decreases by 1.

Can you work out a way to subtract 99 from a number by using place value?

Practise

Use number lines to help solve these:

1 a 55 + 99   b 66 + 99
  c 88 + 99   d 89 + 99

2 a 155 + 99   b 155 + 89
  c 255 + 99   d 255 + 98

3 a 155 − 99   b 266 − 99
  c 366 − 98   d 456 − 99

Try this

Can you work out a similar method to add or subtract 49?

What about adding and subtracting 51?

Explain how understanding place value helps.

Using decimals in measures

Learn

A —————————

B ————————————

C ———————————————

D ——————————————

E ——————————————————————

F ————————————————————————

G —————————————————————————

H —

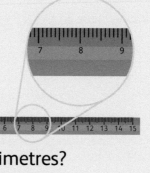

We can use decimals to show numbers between whole numbers. We can write 75 mm as 7.5 cm. 'Centi' means one hundredth, so there are 100 centimetres in a metre. 'Milli' means one thousandth, so there are are 1 000 millimetres in a metre.

Measure line A and line B in millimetres.

Is it easier to write line A or line B in centimetres?

Write 57 mm in centimetres.

Write 9.9 cm in millimetres.

Practise

1 Measure all the lines from the 'Learn' panel in mm and cm.

   For example: A = 30 mm or 3 cm

2 Put these measurements in order, from shortest to longest.

5 cm	45 mm
40 cm	55 mm
2.2 cm	25 mm
31 mm	30 cm
3.2 cm	0.4 cm

Try this

Draw these shapes as accurately as you can:

a A square with sides of 30 mm

b A square with sides of 3.5 cm

c A rectangle with two sides of 45 mm and two sides of 2.1 cm.

Negative numbers

Learn

What temperature is 5° less than 10°?
What temperature is 10° less than 5°?

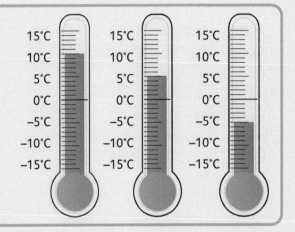

Practise

1 Draw your own thermometer scale from 5° to −5°. Mark all the intervals.
   Use it to work out these temperatures.

   a 5° less than 2°

   b 3° less than 1°

   c 8° less than 5°

   d 10° less than 5°.

2 Look at these temperatures taken around the world:

Place	January	July
New York	−4°	28°
Mexico City	22°	16°
London	2°	19°
Balmaceda	12°	−3°
Mumbai	31°	27°
Helsinki	−9°	14°

   a Which place has the coldest temperature in January?

   b Which place has the coldest temperature in July?

   c Write the places in order of coldest to hottest in January.

Try this

Look at the temperature table again.

Which place has the biggest change in temperature between January and July?

Which has the smallest change?

6b Addition and subtraction

Explore

Key words

number bonds
add
addition
multiple
subtract
subtraction
take away
barrier

How high is this human tower?

Is 100 cm a good estimate?

What about 500 cm?

How could you make a good estimate of the total height?

What factors would you consider to make the best prediction you can?

Number bonds

Learn

Compare these number bond patterns.

1 + 9	1 + 19	11 + 9	1 + 99
2 + 8	2 + 18	12 + 8	2 + 98
3 + 7	3 + 17	13 + 7	3 + 97

What would be the next line in this pattern?
What would be in the tenth line?

> Is it true that the ones digits always sum to 10?

Practise

1 Complete these number bonds.

a
40 + ? = 100
400 + ? = 1 000

b
45 + ? = 100
450 + ? = 1 000

c
100 = 25 + ?
1 000 = 250 + ?

d
? + 30 = 100
? + 300 = 1 000

e
? + 35 = 100
? + 350 = 1 000

f
100 = ? + 20
1 000 = ? + 200

2 The children are running a 1 000 m race.

Name of child	Distance run
Lev	100 m
Maya	150 m
Ace	500 m
Zara	550 m
Felix	800 m
Irina	950 m

How far does each person still have to run? The first one has been done for you.
Lev still has to run:
1 000 m − 100 m = 900 m

3
> The ones digits always add up to 10 when you make a number bond to 100.

Is Lia correct?

Show two different examples to prove that your statement is true.

Write your own statement for what happens to the tens digits in number bonds to 100.

Try this

Use the digits 2, 4, 6, 7 to make number bonds to 100.

How many different solutions can you find?

Now use the digits 2, 5, 5, 7, 0 and 0 to make number bonds to 1 000.

Are there more solutions?

Adding and subtracting multiples of 10

Learn

To play this game, you throw three beanbags onto the target. You add up your three scores.

Sam scored 20, 40 and 70.

Ria scored 40, 20 and 70.

What can we say about their scores?

Practise

1 Write the players in order of their total score, from lowest to highest.

Name	Throw 1	Throw 2	Throw 3
Alec	70	20	10
Lia	90	40	10
Orlando	10	40	40
Afia	90	70	10
Mateo	40	40	40
Nita	90	20	70

2 In the next round, everyone scored exactly 120.

How many different ways are there to score exactly 120 with three throws?

3 Now the scores are changed to numbers that are close to multiples of 10:

White – 89   Blue – 61
Red – 41   Yellow – 39
Green – 19

What is the closest you can score to 150 with exactly three throws?

Try this

Design your own target game so that it is possible to score exactly 100 with three throws, but impossible to score exactly 90.

Using jottings or written methods

Learn

These number lines show how you bridge through a multiple of 100 when adding or subtracting.

Use the number lines to complete the addition and subtraction below.

96 + ? = 103

204 − ? = 195

Practise

1 Draw your own number lines to complete these calculations.
The first one has been done for you.

a 196 + ? = 201

b 203 − ? = 196

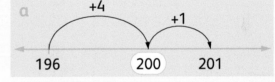

c 494 + ? = 501

d 506 − ? = 499

e ? + 8 = 703

f ? − 7 = 697

2 Use patterns of number bonds to help solve these calculations.

a 14 − 6 = ?

   104 − 6 = ?

   304 − 6 = ?

b 11 − ? = 5

   101 − ? = 95

   301 − ? = 295

c ? − 3 = 9

   ? − 3 = 99

   ? − 3 = 899

3 A road sign says:

Anytown	103 km
Betterville	205 km
Coolton	404 km
Downton	601 km
Everhampton	806 km

How far away will each place be after driving another 7 km?

Try this

Check these calculations by doing an inverse addition.
Which are incorrect?

a 102 − 9 = 94

b 505 − 8 = 397

c 304 − 7 = 297

d 801 − 8 = 793

Adding two-digit numbers

Learn

What strategy would you use to solve 53 + 48: a, b or c?

a 53 = 50 + 3   b 53 + 48 = 53 + 40 + 8 = 93 + 8 = 101
  48 = 40 + 8   c 53 + 48 = 53 + 50 − 2 = 101

  So 53 + 48 = 90 + 11
              = 101

I use partitioning.

Describe to a partner how Lia's method works.

Practise

1 The children recorded how many minutes of TV they watched on Monday and Tuesday. Use estimating to predict whose total is higher than 100.

Name	Monday	Tuesday
Alec	38	92
Lia	24	71
Orlando	48	57
Afia	28	48
Mateo	51	53
Nita	14	41

2 a Work out the exact total time for each person.

  b Write them in order of highest total time to lowest total time.

3 Use the digits on the cards:

Write a pair of two-digit numbers.

Write the total of those two numbers.

What is the highest total you can make with those two numbers?

How many different totals can you make?

Now try the same using these digits:

Try this

Why can you not make a total with an odd answer when you use these cards?

| 6 | 6 | 8 | 8 |

What would happen if you used these digits?

| 5 | 5 | 9 | 9 |

Write an odd total this time. Explain your answer.

Adding and subtracting larger numbers

Learn

3	4	2
		5
		3

Can you see the two different addition methods I used? Which do you prefer? Why?

342 + 253
300 + 40 + 2
200 + 50 + 3
= 500 + 90 + 5
= 595

342 + 253 = 342 + 200 + 50 + 3
= 542 + 50 + 3
= 592 + 3
= 595

Rearrange digits in the diagram to make two different three-digit numbers. Then add the numbers together.

What would the total be if you changed the '4' into a '5'?

Practise

1 Look at these basketball scores.

MATCH A: 116 VS. 132

MATCH B: 141 VS. 128

MATCH C: 123 VS. 125

MATCH D: 135 VS. 116

How many points were scored in total in each match?

Use rounding to check if your answers are sensible. By how many points did the winning team win by in each match?

2 Use the digits 1, 2, 3, 5, 7, 9 to make 2 three-digit numbers to add together.

☐☐☐ + ☐☐☐

What odd totals can you make?

Where do you have to put the '2' if you want to make an odd total?

3 Use the digits 1, 2, 3, 5, 7.

What odd totals can you make?

Where do you have to put the '2' if you want to make an odd total?

Think like a mathematician

When you are trying to make a specific target, try changing one digit at a time.

Subtracting two-digit and three-digit numbers

Learn

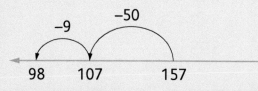

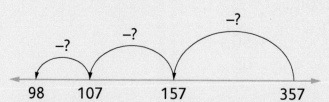

Use the number lines to work out the missing information in these subtractions:

157 − ? = 98

357 − ? = 98

Practise

1 I started with a piece of ribbon that was 800 cm long.

Each time I cut a piece of ribbon, my piece of ribbon gets shorter and shorter. I cut the following lengths off:

a 12 cm   b 123 cm

c 99 cm   d 250 cm

e 101 cm   f 149 cm

The first one has been done for you.

a I would have 800 cm − 12 cm = 788 cm.

How much would I have left at the end?

2 Write your own story problems for these subtractions:

a A three-digit number subtract a one-digit number

b A three-digit number subtract a two-digit number

c A three-digit number subtract a three-digit number.

Be ready to share your stories with the class.

Try this

Look at these subtractions: 321 − 123

Explain any patterns you notice.   432 − 234

Do not work out the answers yet.   543 − 345

Predict which of the subtractions will have an answer that:

a ends in a zero

b is less than 100

c is between 200 and 300

d is an even number.

Now check by doing the calculations.

Self-check

A Number and the number system

1 Partition these numbers. Do each one in two different ways.
   a 2001
   b 2100
   c 2121

2 Round these numbers to the nearest 10.
   a 1111
   b 3333
   c 5555
   d 7777

3 Convert these measurements to cm.
   a 33 mm
   b 50 mm
   c 77 mm
   d 90 mm

4 Write three temperatures that are below 0°.

B Addition and subtraction

Solve the following calculations:

1 $50 + 40 + 60 = ?$

2 $555 - 101 = ?$

3 $? + 950 = 1000$

4 Lia had 306c, but she spent 8c. How much money did she have left?

5 $123 + 234 = ?$

6 $234 - 123 = ?$

7 What is the smallest total you can make by using the digits 2, 5, 4, and 7 to make 2 two-digit numbers?

Unit 7   Measures and problem solving

7a The metric system

Explore

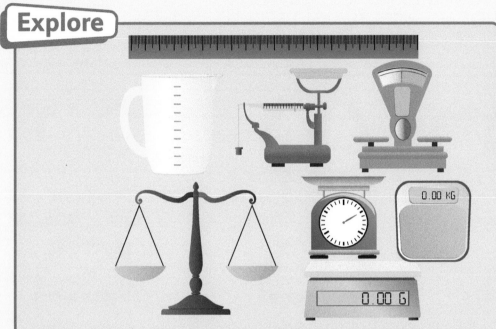

Key words
mass
weight
gram
kilogram
measure
balance

What is the same and what is different about these measuring devices?

Which would you use to measure the mass of an apple?

Which would you use to compare the weights of different items?

Which could weigh up to 50 kg?

Which could measure very small weights?

Converting grams and kilograms

Learn

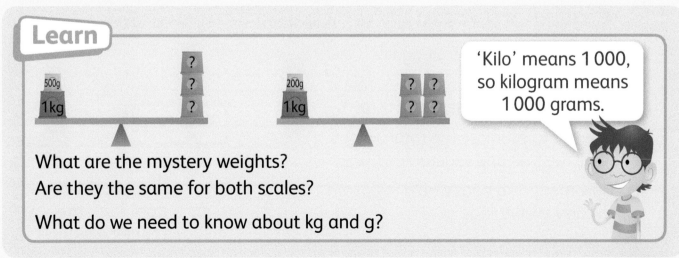

'Kilo' means 1 000, so kilogram means 1 000 grams.

What are the mystery weights?

Are they the same for both scales?

What do we need to know about kg and g?

Practise

1 Estimate the weight shown on these scales.
  Write your answers in grams. The first one has been done for you.

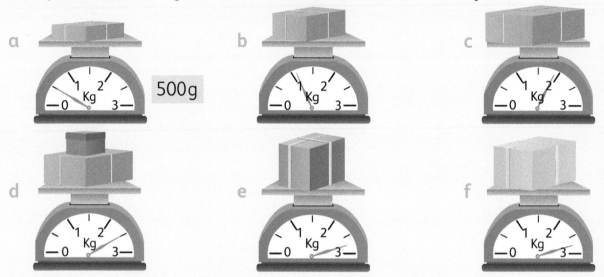

a 500g

b

c

d

e

f

2 Here are some weights of items from the supermarket.

   a Write the total weight of these
      items. The first one has been
      done for you.
      ● apples and pineapple
         350g + 625g = 975g
      ● oranges and mango
      ● bananas and oranges
      ● potatoes and mango.

   b I can only carry 1 kg in my bag.
      What three items could I buy?

Bag of apples	350 g
Pineapple	625 g
Bag of potatoes	740 g
Oranges	275 g
Bananas	538 g
Mango	188 g

3 Look at the weights of fruit again.

   a For all the fruit and vegetables, round
      each weight to the nearest 100 g.

   b Use this to estimate the total weight
      of all the fruit and vegetables.

   c How many 1 kg bags would you need
      to carry everything?

Try this

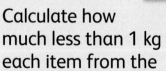

Calculate how
much less than 1 kg
each item from the
supermarket weighs.

7b Length, area and perimeter

Key words ⟳
length
decimal
centimetre
metre
area
perimeter

Explore

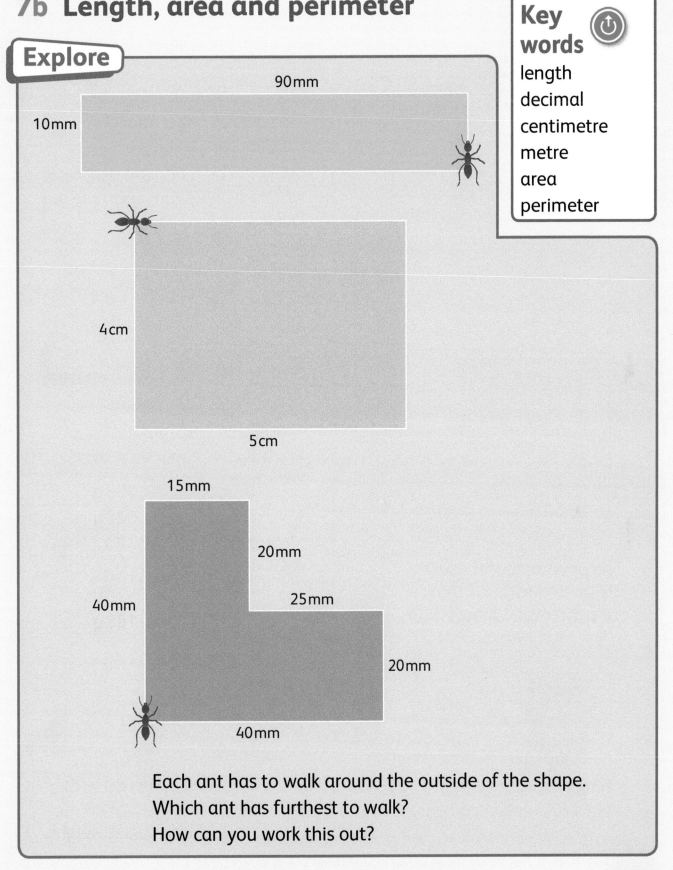

Each ant has to walk around the outside of the shape.

Which ant has furthest to walk?

How can you work this out?

* These drawings on this page are drawn smaller
and do not show the actual size of a cm.

Squares and rectangles

Learn

5 cm

5 cm

10 cm

10 cm

The perimeter of these is 20 cm and 40 cm. I think their perimeter is larger than their area.

Do you agree?

Practise

1 On squared paper, draw five different size squares.

Write the area and the perimeter of each square. One example has been done for you.

Perimeter = 5 + 5 + 5 + 5 = 20 cm

Area = 5 × 5 = 25 squares

Is it always true that the area is a bigger number than the perimeter?

Whenever I draw a square, the perimeter is always an even number.

2 a Do you agree? Why?

b Is the area always an even number?

3 Draw a rectangle where the perimeter is an odd number.

* These drawings on this page are drawn smaller and do not show the actual size of a cm.

Using decimals in perimeter problems

Learn

How could you work out the perimeter of the stamp?
Convert the measurements to millimetres, then use addition.

2.1 cm

1.5 cm

Practise

1 Which of these rectangles has a perimeter of less than 10 cm?

Rectangle	Width	Height
A	2.1 cm	1.9 cm
B	1.9 cm	3.2 cm
C	2.5 cm	2.4 cm
D	2.3 cm	2.8 cm
E	4.4 cm	1 cm
F	9 mm	1.1 cm

2 If you have 14 cm of string, can you make a square outline?

What if you have 10 cm?

3 Design three different rectangles with a perimeter greater than 9 cm but less than 10 cm.

Think like a mathematician

If you convert the centimetres into millimetres, it gives you another way to solve these problems.

Try this

Design three different squares with a perimeter greater than 9 cm, but less than 10 cm.

7c Time

Explore

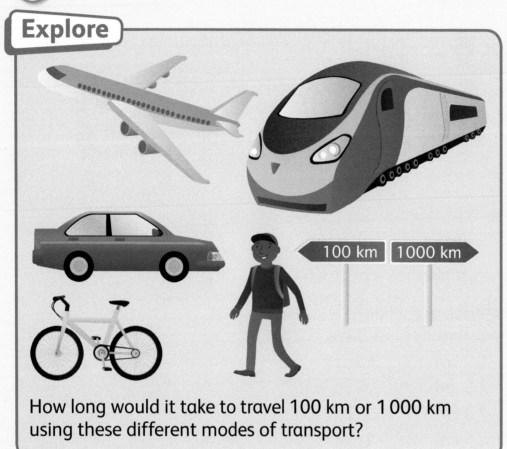

Key words

a.m.

p.m.

hour

minute

o'clock

timetable

analogue

digital

How long would it take to travel 100 km or 1000 km using these different modes of transport?

Reasoning about timetables

Learn

Leaves from	Bus A	Bus B	Bus C	Bus D	Bus E
Bus depot	9.00 a.m.	10.30 a.m.	12.00 noon	1.30 p.m.	?
Hotel	9.20 a.m.	10.50 a.m.	12.20 p.m.	?	?
Train station	9.45 a.m.	11.15 a.m.	12.45 p.m.	?	?
Town centre	10.05 a.m.	11.35 a.m.	1.05 p.m.	?	?
Hospital	10.23 a.m.	11.53 a.m.	1.23 p.m.	?	?
Supermarket	10.40 a.m.	12.10 p.m.	1.40 p.m.	?	4.40 p.m.

What time does Bus B leave the train station?

Practise

1 Use the timetable to answer the following questions. The first one has been done for you.

   a What time does Bus A leave the hospital? 10.23 a.m.

   b When does Bus B start its journey?

   c How long does it take Bus C to drive from the Train station to the Town Centre?

   d How long is the journey for Bus A from the Town Centre to the hospital?

   e Does Bus A travel at the same speed as Bus B and Bus C? How can you tell?

2 The information is missing for Bus D and Bus E.

   a Find the times that are missing from the timetable.

   b The last bus of the day is Bus F. Calculate the times Bus F will arrive at each location.

3 Lia lives near the Bus depot. She needs to get to the hospital by midday.

   a Which bus should she catch?

   b How long would her journey take her?

   c If she took Bus A, how long would she have to wait at the hospital?

4 Alec lives near the hotel. It takes him 12 minutes to walk from his house to the bus stop at the hotel. He needs to meet his brother at the train station at 3.00 p.m. He has just finished his lunch. This is the time on his clock at home:

   Will Alec be able to meet his brother at the right time?

Try this

Create your own story problems about the bus timetable. Write three problems: easy, medium and difficult. Write them neatly on a piece of paper so you can display them in class for other people to solve.

7d Problem solving

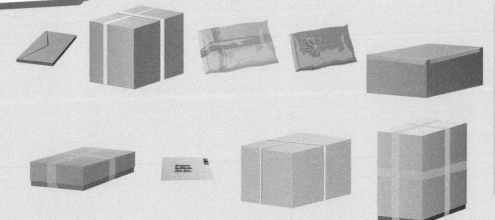

Package A = 111 g
Package B = 222 g
Package C = 333 g
Package D = 444 g
Package E = 555 g
Package F = 666 g
Package G = 777 g
Package H = 888 g
Package I = 999 g

Can you work out which package is which, by looking at the picture?

Do you have to make any estimates, or can you tell for sure?

Try this

What is a good estimate for the total weight of all the packages?

Key words

solve
problem
estimate
explain
reason

Rounding, estimating and explaining

Learn

I weighed packages A, B, C and D at the same time. I think the scales might be broken.

Use rounding to check if Nia's weighing scales are broken.

Practise

1 You go shopping. You fetch one package from the post office and one item of food from the shop.

Which package and food item could you carry together in one plastic bag if the maximum weight a plastic bag can carry is 1 kg?

Package A	= 111 g
Package B	= 222 g
Package C	= 333 g
Package D	= 444 g
Package E	= 555 g
Package F	= 666 g
Package G	= 777 g
Package H	= 888 g
Package I	= 999 g

340 g

250 g

110 g

220 g

The first one has been done for you.

Eggs + package H $110 g + 888 g = 998 g$

2 Another bag can carry up to 2 kg.

Use rounding to predict 3 different packages you could carry at once.

How many solutions can you find?

3 Work out what to add to each package to make the total weight:

Package A + ? weigh 200 g

Package B + ? weigh 300 g

Package C + ? weigh 400 g

Continue this pattern until you reach Package I.

4 Discuss and write your own story problem to do with the weight of these packages.
Decide on your favourite problem to share with the class.

Self-check

A **The metric system**

1 How many grams is 3 kg?

2 Is 350 g + 450 g + 500 g more or less than $1\frac{1}{2}$ kg?

3 Draw a scale from 2 kg to 3 kg to show 2 200 g and 2 900 g.

B **Length, area and perimeter**

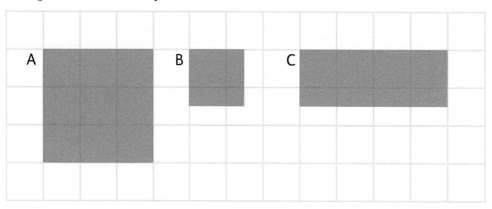

1 Find the area of square A.

2 Find the perimeter of square B.

3 Find the area and perimeter of rectangle C.

C **Time**

1 A train leaves the station at 11.45 a.m. and arrives at the swimming pool 40 minutes later. What time did it arrive?

2 A bus arrived at the swimming pool at 12.25 p.m. The journey took 35 minutes. What time did it leave?

Unit 8   Number and problem solving

8a Number patterns

Explore

1	2	3	4	5	6	7
8	9	10	11	12	13	14
15	16	17	18	19	20	21
22	23	24	25	26	27	28
29	30	31	32	33	34	35
36	37	38	39	40	41	42
43	44	45	46	47	48	49
50	51	52	53	54	55	56
57	58	59	60	61	62	63
64	65	66	67	68	69	70
71	72	73	74	75	76	77
78	79	80	81	82	83	84
85	86	87	88	89	90	91
92	93	94	95	96	97	98
99	100					

1	2	3	4	5	6	7	8
9	10	11	12	13	14	15	16
17	18	19	20	21	22	23	24
25	26	27	28	29	30	28	32
33	34	35	36	37	38	39	40
41	42	43	44	45	46	47	48
49	50	51	52	53	54	55	56
57	58	59	60	61	62	63	64
65	66	67	68	69	70	71	72
73	74	75	76	77	78	79	80
81	82	83	84	85	86	87	88
89	90	91	92	93	94	95	96
97	98	99	100				

Key words
multiple
sequence
increase
decrease

What is the same and what is different in these number grids?
Would 100 be highlighted in either grid?
What numbers greater than 100 would be highlighted?

Learn

Look at the number patterns in the 'Explore' panel.
Which numbers are odd and which are even?
What happens when you add an odd number to an even number?

Odd and even sequences

Practise

1 Predict which of these calculations will have an odd or an even answer.

Check, then sort them into two groups: odd and even answers.

a 22 + 15   b 25 + 14

c 15 + 9   d 19 + 5

e 25 + 22   f 25 + 29

g 129 + 25   h 299 + 22

i 159 + 125   j 195 + 125

2 Will the next number in these sequences be odd or even?

a 5, 10, 15, 20, 25, 30, ?

b 10, 20, 30, 40, 50, ?

c 800, 700, 600, 500, ?

d 48, 45, 42, ?

e 48, 44, 40, ?

f 28, 32, 36, ?

What can you say about the 10th number in each sequence. The 100th?

3 What would be the next square with an even number?

a 555 550 545 540 535 530

b 550 545 540 535 530 525

c 170 175 180 185 190 195

d 303 306 309 312 315 318

e 444 448 452 456 460 464

f 969 966 963 960 957 954

Think like a mathematician

You can work out if any number is odd or even, just by looking at the ones digit. If it is 1, 3, 5 or 7, then the number must be odd.

Try this

For each of the sequences in Q3, work out whether the 10th shape would be a circle, square or triangle.

Then work out if it would be an odd or even number.

Would the 10th circle be odd or even?

Would the 100th square be odd or even.

How do you know?

Increasing and decreasing sequences

Learn

If we input 1 111 into these function machines, we get these outputs:

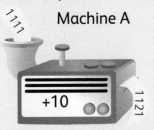
Machine A

Machine B

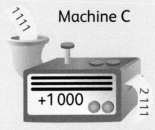
Machine C

1 111 + 10 = 1 121   1 111 − 100 = 1 011   1 111 + 1 000 = 2 111

What would the output be for the inputs: 1 234, 2 345 and 3 456? Which digits would change each time?

The −100 machine changes the hundreds digit only: 1 2̲34 −100 = 1 1̲34.

Practise

1 Work out the output for each function machine if the input is:

   a 3 333   b 4 444   c 3 344   d 4 433   e 9 090   f 1 001

2 Work out the rule for each sequence and write the next three numbers.

   a 11, 21, 31, 41, 51, …   b 51, 56, 61, 66, 71, …   c 115, 119, 123, …

   d 24, 44, 64, …

   e 224, 424, 624, …

   f 8 824, 8 624, 8 424, …

   g 8 110, 7 110, 6 110, …

Try this

Invent sequences that:

a decrease and contain the numbers 50 and 20, but not 40 and 30

b increase and contain the numbers 200 and 300, but not 250.

8b Multiplication and division

Explore

There are two traffic lights at every crossroads. How could you calculate how many traffic lights are needed?

How many cars would there be if there were ten cars waiting at each set of lights?

Doubling, halving and using the 2× table

Learn

Look at these patterns.

$12 \times 2 = 20 + 4$	$26 \times 2 = 40 + 12$	$19 \ \times 2 = 20 + 18$
$22 \times 2 = 40 + 4$	$36 \times 2 = ? \ + ?$	$190 \times 2 = 200 + 180$
$32 \times 2 = ? + ?$	$? \ \times 2 = 80 + 12$	$29 \ \times 2 = ? + ?$
		$290 \times 2 = ? + ?$

Can you think how to find the missing information?

Key words
double
half
halve
times table
multiply
divide
inverse

Practise

1 Copy and complete these calculations. The first one has been done for you.

a Double 15 = 20 + 10
   Double 25 = 40 + ?
   Double 35 = ? + ?

b Double 150 = 200 + ?
   Double 250 = 400 + ?
   Double 350 = ? + ?

c $? \times 2 = 240$
   $? \times 2 = 440$
   $? \times 2 = 640$
   $? \times 2 = 840$

d $? \times 2 = 28$
   $? \times 2 = 48$
   $? \times 2 = 280$
   $? \times 2 = 480$

2 It costs $2 a ticket to go to the fairground.
   How much money was taken at the gate on the following days?
   Monday – 35 people   Tuesday – 45 people
   Wednesday – 49 people   Thursday – 80 people
   Friday – 130 people

3 The following week, the fairground took these amounts at the gate each day:
   Monday – $120   Tuesday – $180   Wednesday – $150
   Thursday – $190   Friday – $210
   How many tickets did they sell on each day?

Try this

I think of a number. I double it, add 20, and halve the result. The answer is 25. What was my number?

I think of a number. I add 20, then I double it. I subtract 20, and then halve the result. The answer is 25. What was my number?

The 4×, 5× and 10× tables

Learn

Arrays show multiplication and division facts.
How many different calculations can you 'see' in this array?
These calculations could be 5 × 4, or 4 × 5.
You can choose the order of multiplications to make them easier to solve.

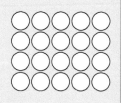

Practise

1 Use the array to answer these questions:

　a What multiplications would it show if you added another red column?

　b What multiplications would it show if you took away a yellow column?

　c What would you have to do to make it show 5 × 5?

　d How many red dots and how many yellow dots will there be in a 4 × 7 array? Draw your own to check your prediction.

2 The children have been saving money every week.

Lia saves $10. Alec saves $5. Orlando saves $4.

　a Compare how much more Alec has than Orlando after five weeks, ten weeks and 20 weeks.

　b Compare how much more Lia has than Alec after five weeks, ten weeks and 20 weeks.

　c Predict how much more Lia would have than Orlando after 100 weeks.

Try this

Lia, Alec and Orlando want to join their money together to buy a radio-controlled car that costs $150.

How many weeks do they need to save?

The 3×, 6× and 9× tables

Learn

How can 3 × 3 help you work out 3 × 6 and 3 × 9?

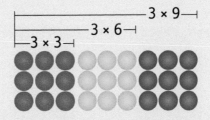

Practise

1 Draw an array to show 2 × 3, 2 × 6 and 2 × 9 in the same diagram.

2 Complete these families of facts.

a
3 × 1 = ☐
6 × 1 = ☐
9 × 1 = ☐

b
3 × 4 = ☐
6 × 4 = ☐
9 × 4 = ☐

c
3 × ☐ = 21
6 × ☐ = 42
9 × ☐ = 63

d
24 = ☐ × 3
48 = ☐ × 6
72 = ☐ × 9

3 Write a **division** fact from the 3×, 6× or 9× tables to solve each of these problems. Calculate how many children there were in a group each time:

a There were 27 children at a party, and they sat in nine equal groups.

b There were 27 children, but three left. The rest sat in four equal groups.

c There were 36 children at a party, and they sat in nine equal groups.

d There were 33 children at a party, and they sat in three equal groups.

e There were 35 children, but five left. The rest sat in five equal groups.

Try this

Are the following statements always, sometimes, or never true?

a If you add two multiples of 3, you get a multiple of 3.

b If you add two multiples of 3 you get a multiple of 6.

c If you add two multiples of 6 you get a multiple of 9.

d If you subtract a multiple of 3 from a multiple of 10, you get a multiple of 6.

Convince your partner using examples and explaining your reasons.

Multiplying one-digit and two-digit numbers

Learn

How can you work out the answer to these multiplications?
Do these hints help?   30 × 5 = ? and 2 × 5 = ?

A

30 × 5 = 150

2 × 5 = 10

So 32 × 5 = 150 + 10 = 160

Practise

1 Rearrange the cards from 'A' in the 'Learn' panel to make six different multiplications. You must use each card once in each multiplication.

   Put the multiplications in order, based on the size of the answer.

2 Rearrange the cards of set B to make some new multiplications.

   How many odd answers and how many even answers can you find?

   B

3 Make new multiplications by rearranging the cards in set C and D.

   C   D

   Predict whether set C or set D will have more odd answers.

   Try a few different examples to see if your prediction is right.

Try this

Write a rule for what happens when you:
a multiply an even number by an even number
b multiply an odd number by an odd number.

Checking and explaining

Learn

It costs $3 to buy a stationery set for one pupil. How much does it cost for a class of 32 pupils?

Is Sanjay right?

What mistake did he make?

Are there other methods for solving Sanjay's problem?

Explain which method you would choose, and why?

I got the answer $150, but it seems too big. 30 × 3 is only $90 if I round to the nearest 10.

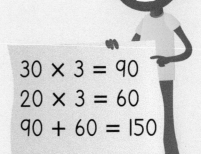

$$30 \times 3 = 90$$
$$20 \times 3 = 60$$
$$90 + 60 = 150$$

Practise

1 Write a multiplication to find the correct cost for Sanjay.

2 Class 1 has three plum trees. Each tree had between 70 and 80 plums.
Class 2 has five pear trees. Each tree had between 30 and 40 pears.
Class 3 has seven apple trees. Each tree had between 20 and 30 apples.
Class 4 has nine fig trees. Each tree had between 15 and 25 figs.

Make an estimate of how much fruit each class grew.

Class 1 grew between ☐ and ☐ plums.

Which class do you think grew the most fruit? Why?

3 Write a story problem that has a multiplication with an answer between:

a 100 and 150
b 150 and 200
c 500 and 600
d 800 and 900.

Suggest a method you could use to solve each problem.

Dividing two-digit numbers

Learn

What is the same and what is different about these missing number problems?

$7 \times \boxed{} = 70$

$8 \times \boxed{} = 80$

$7 \times \boxed{} = 77$

$8 \times \boxed{} = 88$

$\boxed{} \times 12 = 96$

$\boxed{} \times 12 = 84$

$70 \div \boxed{} = 7$

$80 \div \boxed{} = 8$

$77 \div 7 = \boxed{}$

$88 \div 8 = \boxed{}$

$\boxed{} \div 12 = 7$

$\boxed{} \div 12 = 8$

Try this

Find three different numbers that can be divided by these pairs of numbers without leaving a remainder:

a 3 and 5

b 4 and 5

c 6 and 5

d 4 and 7

Practise

1 Find the missing numbers. The first one has been done for you.

a $3 \times 11 = \boxed{33}$

b $3 \times \boxed{} = 39$

c $4 \times \boxed{} = 48$

d $4 \times \boxed{} = 52$

e $\boxed{} \times 11 = 22$

f $\boxed{} \times 13 = 26$

g $\boxed{} \times 20 = 60$

h $3 \times \boxed{} = 63$

2 Here are the learner numbers at a school. Each stage needs to be split into groups of 3 for Sports Day, and into groups of 4 for the lunch tables.

a How many groups of 3 are there for each stage?

b How many groups of 4 are there for each stage?

c Which stage could also be split into groups of 5?

Stage	Learners
Stage 1	24
Stage 2	48
Stage 3	60
Stage 4	72
Stage 5	96

Division with remainders

Learn

I need 63 balloons for my Grandmother's 63rd birthday party. The balloons come in packs of 6.

I have baked 63 cupcakes for the party. I can fit 6 cakes on a plate. How many plates will be full?

How many packs should Alec buy?

How can he make sure he has enough?

What division calculation goes with this problem?

What is the same and what is different about how you have to answer Lia's question?

1 Alec finds balloons from different shops.

Packs of 3 = $2   Packs of 5 = $3

Packs of 6 = $4   Packs of 10 = $7

How many of each pack could he buy?

Which is the cheapest option?

2 Lia has found different size plates. How many of each plate could Lia use to put out her 63 cakes? Find three different ways she can do this.

8c Problem solving

Explore

How many different multiplications and divisions can go with each array?

Why are there not four different multiplication and division facts for each array?

Key words

array

square

square number

Remainders and arrays

Learn

You can make a square array by using nine counters. If you use ten counters you cannot make a square.

Is it possible to make a square using 15 or 16 counters? Convince your partner.

Practise

1 On squared paper, draw some different square arrays. Write a multiplication and a division to go with each array. The first one has been done for you.

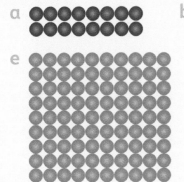

$5 \times 5 = 25$ $25 \div 5 = 5$

2 Which of these arrays can be rearranged to form a square?

a 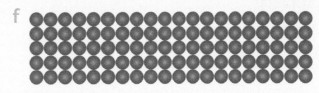   b    c   d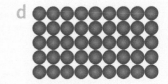

e

f

3 Oranges are packed in trays.

Each tray has six rows of six oranges.
Then six trays are stacked in a box.

How many oranges are there in a box?

Try this

How many different square arrays can you see in each diagram? Remember to look for squares of different sizes.

A   B   C

Self-check

A **Number patterns**

1 Would the answer to this be odd or even: 205 + 15?

2 Write the three next numbers: 161, 171, 181, ⬚, ⬚, ⬚

3 Write the missing numbers: 3 999, ⬚, 5 999, ⬚, 7 999, ⬚

B **Multiplication and division**

1 What number do you have to double to make 72?

2 What number is half of 82?

3 Which of these has the greatest answer?

    a 3 × 9   b 4 × 6

    c 5 × 5   d 2 × 10

4 Sort these in order, from smallest to greatest.

    a 13 × 5   b 14 × 3   c 12 × 6.

5 Write a division that gives the same answer as 84 ÷ 4.

6 Write the remainder for these:

    a 84 ÷ 3   b 65 ÷ 9   c 99 ÷ 8

7 These calculations have been used to check the answers to division story problems.

    a 4 × 15   b 5 × 18

    c 3 × 31   d 7 × 13

Write the division and a story problem for each answer.

⟳ 9a Handling data

Explore

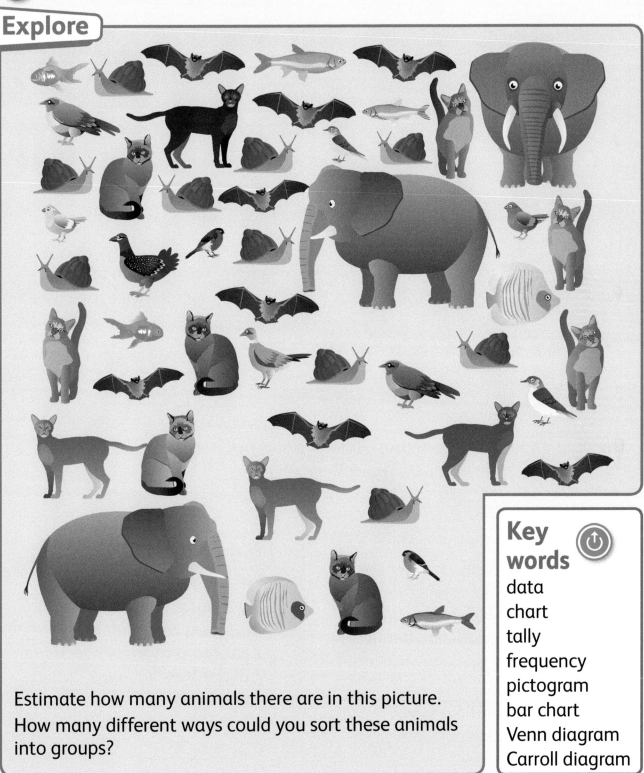

Estimate how many animals there are in this picture.

How many different ways could you sort these animals into groups?

Key words ⟳
data
chart
tally
frequency
pictogram
bar chart
Venn diagram
Carroll diagram

Tally charts, pictograms and frequency tables

Learn

Number of legs	Tally	Frequency
0	IIII IIII IIII II	
1		
2	IIII IIII IIII III	
3	IIII	
4	IIII IIII	

How they move		
Fly		▢▢▢▢
Walk		▢▢▢▢
Swim		▢▢
Slither		▢▢▢▢▢▢▢▢▢

Key
▢ = 4 animals

The data about animals in the 'Explore' panel has not been accurately counted. Check the numbers yourself.

Practise

1 Draw your own tally chart for the number of animal legs in the 'Explore' panel on page 103. Make sure you give the correct data and frequencies.

2 Draw your own pictogram for the ways the animals move. Look carefully at the key and draw your symbols accurately.

Try this

Draw your own selection of 20 different animals. Create your own tally chart and pictogram to show how many have stripes and how many have spots.

Bar charts

Learn

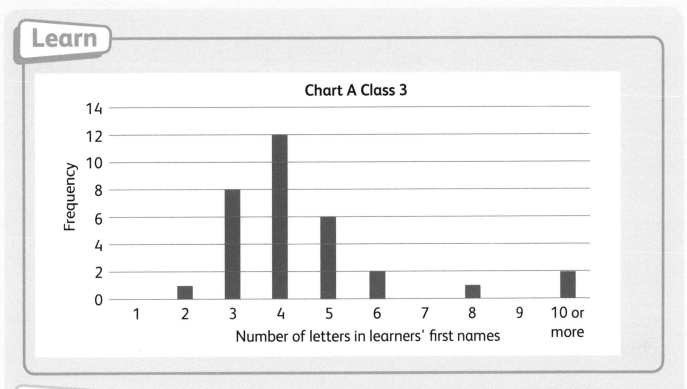

Chart A Class 3

Frequency (y-axis: 0, 2, 4, 6, 8, 10, 12, 14)

Number of letters in learners' first names (x-axis: 1, 2, 3, 4, 5, 6, 7, 8, 9, 10 or more)

Practise

1 Look at Chart A and answer these questions. The first one has been done for you.

a How many people have six letters in their name?
   2 people have 6 letters in their name.

b What is the most common length of a name?

c How many people have more than five letters in their name?

d How many people have less than four letters in their name?

e How many people are in Class 3?

Try this

Create your own bar chart for name length in your class.

Compare your results with Class 3.

Write the main similarities and differences.

Think carefully about the scale you will use to draw it.

In our class, only two learners have three-letter names.

Learn

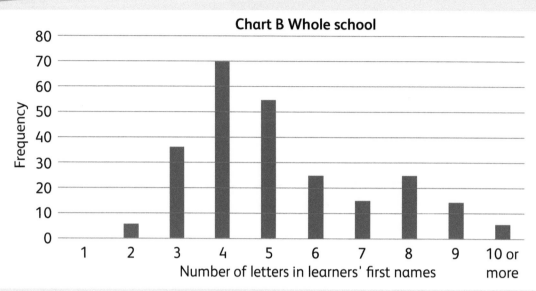

What is the same and what is different about this chart and Chart A (on page 105)?

Practise

1 Look at Chart B and answer the following questions:
   a How many people have five letters in their name?
   b How many people have more than six letters in their name?
   c How many people have fewer than five letters in their name?
   d How many people are in the whole school?
   e How many more people have four letters than six letters in their name?

2 Look at Charts A and B and say if the following statements are true or false. (Remember that Class 3 is part of the whole school.)
   a There are more than 200 people who are not in Class 3.
   b In Class 3, five-letter names are more common than three-letter names, but in the whole school it is the other way around.
   c All of the people who have two letters in their name are in Class 3.
   d There are more people in Class 3 that have ten letters or more than in the rest of the school.

Venn and Carroll diagrams

Learn

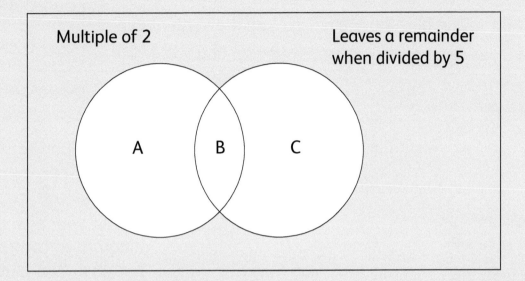

	Multiple of 2	Not a multiple of 2
Remainder when divided by 5	D	E
No remainder when divided by 5	F	G

Where would the number 11 go in each diagram?

Think of a number to go in section B, and a number to go in section G.

Practise

1 Find three numbers to go in each section of the Venn diagram.

Find three numbers that do not go into the Venn diagram.

2 Find three numbers to go in each section of the Carroll diagram.

Do not repeat any numbers from question one.

3 Look at this Carroll diagram.

	Multiple of 3	Not a multiple of 3
Remainder when divided by 3		
No remainder when divided by 3		

Explain why some sections will always remain empty.

Try this

Create your own Carroll diagram to compare numbers that leave remainders when you divide by 4 and when you divide by 5.

Find three numbers to go in each section.

Self-check

A **Handling data**

1 What is the difference between a pictogram and a tally chart?

2 What is the difference between a bar chart and a pictogram?

3 Copy the Carroll diagram above. Sort these numbers into the correct sections: 21, 23, 42, 81, 27, 35.

9b Problem solving

Explore

What is the difference between the blue and red spotted starfish?
Think of two different ways to count the spots in the tank.
Which way would a mathematician choose?

Key words
list
table
systematic
true
false

Being systematic

Learn

I have spotted starfish as pets. In my tank there are 25 spots in total.

How many blue and red spotted starfish might Lia have?

How could this table help?

Number of fish	Number of red spots	Number of blue spots
…	5	4
…	10	8
…	15	12
…	20	16
…	…	20

Practise

1 Alec says that there are 30 spots in total in his tank.

How many blue and red spotted starfish might Alec have?

Write two different solutions.

2 In Orlando's tank there are 40 spots, and in Irina's tank there are 50 spots.

Who has the most possible combinations of each type of starfish?

3 Felix adds together three different whole numbers to make a total of 20.

Write all the possible solutions.

How can you be sure you have found all the solutions?

Try this

What different numbers less than 30 is it **impossible** to make by adding a multiple of 3, a multiple of 4 and a multiple of 5?

Deciding if a statement is true or false

Learn

When you divide a number by two, you get an answer that ends in a zero.

Is that true?

Try some calculations.

How would we know if it was always, sometimes or never true?

Practise

1 True or False? For each false statement, write a true one.

   a Rectangles have an odd number of right angles.

   b Squares have fewer corners than pentagons.

   c Triangles can have three right angles.

   d Pentagons have six sides.

   e Octagons are not 3-D shapes.

   f Squares are symmetrical.

2 Find three examples and three counter-examples for each statement. The first one has been done for you.

   a When you add two numbers, you get an odd answer.

Three examples for the statement	Three counter examples (against the statement)
15 + 16 = 31	4 + 2 = 6
5 + 7 = 23	12 + 8 = 20
6 + 9 = 15	11 + 9 = 30

   b When you multiply two numbers, you get an even answer.

   c When you add two multiples of 3 you get a multiple of 10.

   d When you divide a number by 5, you get a remainder of 4.

111

Think like a mathematician

When you add two numbers, you get an answer ending in a 5.

For	Against
4 + 1	3 + 1
14 + 1	13 + 1
24 + 11	23 + 11

You can collect your examples in a table, like this, to show if they support, or go against the statement.

Finding all solutions

Learn

What numbers could you make by rearranging the cards?

How many different numbers can you make using each card once?

Here is Lia's way of ordering her solutions:

234	324	423
243	343	?

She is missing one solution. What is it?

How could Lia be sure she had found all the possible solutions?

Practise

1
| 2 | 6 | 8 |

Write all the different numbers you can make using each card once. The first one has been done for you. 268

2 Use the digits 2, 6 and 8 again, but this time you are allowed to repeat a digit.

 a How many two-digit numbers can you write?

 b How many three-digit numbers can you write?

3
| 1 | 2 | 3 | 4 |

Can you make more odd or more even numbers by using each card once?

4 Each boat must have a cabin, a sail and a window. These are the different features that boats can have.

Boat feature	Types			
Window	square	round		
Cabin	triangular	round	square	
Sail types	plain	spotty	striped	zigzagged

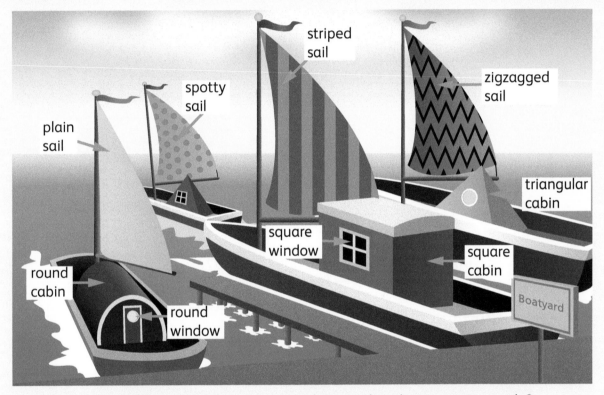

a How many different boats can you design that have spotty sails?
b How many different boats can you design that have triangular cabins?
c How many different boats can you design that have square windows?

Try this

Estimate how many combinations there are in total, for all the different boats you can build. You have already found many of them in Question 4.
Now develop a system to help you find them all.

Buying boats

Learn

A boat needs windows, cabins and a sail. Here is a price list for these options.

Boat part	Price
Windows	Round = $120 Square = $110
Cabins	Triangular = $430 Square = $450 Round = $480
Sails	Plain = $215 Striped = $225 Spotty = $235 Zigzagged = $245

Practise

1 Orlando's grandmother wants to buy a new boat. She has $1 000. How much change will she get if she buys a boat with these features?

2 Felix's Uncle wants to buy a boat, but he has only saved $770.

What different styles of boat can he buy?

3 What is the most expensive boat and the least expensive boat?

What is the difference in price between the two?

Try this

Can you design a boat that costs an exact multiple of $100? Explain your answer.

Unit 10 Problem solving and review

10a Problem solving

Explore

Key words
estimate
predict
solve
puzzle
pattern

Picture problems

1 Estimate how many people live in the village.

Give reasons for your estimates, including how many people you estimate live in each house.

2 How long do you estimate it would take to travel from the village to the foot of the snowy mountains by:

   a walking **b** car **c** boat.

Explain your estimations.

3 Estimate the height of the mountains.

Give reasons for your estimates.

Try this

Look carefully at the photo of the village.

What clues are there about the time of day and the time of year? Give a prediction of the month and time of day this photograph was taken, with reasons for your prediction.

Compare your reasons with a partner. Convince him or her that you are correct.

Story problems

This table shows the prices for travelling on a boat from the village to the mountains.

Season	Time	Adult	Child
Winter	January–March	$9	$5
Spring	April–June	$12	$8
Summer	July–September	$15	$11
Autumn	October–December	$6	$2

1 One day in winter, $55 of tickets are sold. How many adults and children could have bought tickets?

Write two solutions.

2 How much more does it cost this family to travel to the mountains in summer than in winter?

3 This family take the boat once in each season.

Do they spend more than $100 over the year?

If so, how much?

If not, how much change would they get from $100?

4 On one day in winter, the same amount is spent on adult tickets as child tickets. How much did they sell in total?

Story problems

When the children reach the snowy part of the mountain, they find a snowman.

There are four different hats, three different scarves, and a carrot or an orange for a nose.

1 How many different ways can they finish the snowman so that the hat is a different colour from the scarf?

2 How many different ways can they finish the snowman if the hat and the scarf can be the same colour?

3 Try to work out whose snowman is whose by using these clues.

a   b   c   d

- Lia's snowman has a yellow hat, but a different colour scarf.
- Orlando's snowman has the same colour hat and scarf.
- Alec's snowman has a carrot for a nose.
- Lia's and Orlando's snowmen have the same nose.
- Felix's has the same colour scarf as Orlando.

Think like a mathematician

When you are solving problems with lots of solutions, it is a good idea to organise your ideas. For example, try drawing snowmen with the same hat in one line, and change the scarf each time.

Number and calculation problems

Here is a list of some mountain heights from around the world.

Mountain	Height in metres (m)
Mauna Kea	4 205 m
Mont Blanc	4 809 m
Everest	8 848 m
Aconagua	6 962 m
Mount Fuji	3 776 m
Ben Nevis	1 345 m

Mauna Kea

1 List the mountains in order of height, from smallest to tallest.

2 Round each height to the nearest 100 m.

3 Which mountain is approximately 5 000 m shorter than Everest?

4 The tallest mountain on the planet Mars, called Olympus Mons, is twice as tall as Mount Everest. Use rounding to approximate the height of this mountain.

Try this

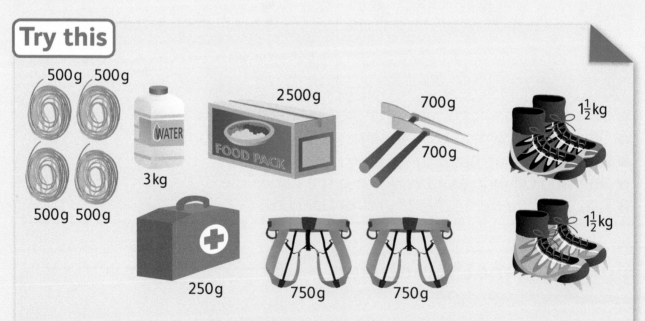

Two climbers want to share the equipment equally between them.

Work out the best way to share the equipment so that they carry a fair amount each.

Unit 11 Number and problem solving

⏻ 11a Numbers and the number system

Explore

How would the temperatures be different at different places in this picture?

Where would be the hottest place?

What would be the coldest?

Money and decimals

Learn

Which of these prices is nearest to $5?
What is $2.49 rounded to the nearest dollar?
What is each price tag in cents?
Put the prices in order from smallest to biggest.

$4.92 $5.09

$1.51 $2.90 $5.60

$0.51 $0.49

Practise

1 Round all of the price tags in the 'Learn' panel to the nearest dollar. The first one has been done for you. $4.92 rounds to $5

2 Round each amount on the menu to the nearest dollar, to help work out what each person bought.

Menu
Juice — 99c
Coffee — $1.89
Sandwich — $3.75
Pizza — $7.99

   a Alec bought two items and spent about $6

   b Lia bought two items and spent about $5

   c Orlando bought two items and spent nearly $10

   d Felix bought three items and spent nearly $7

   e Maya bought three items and spent nearly $11

   f Ace bought three items and spent nearly $14.

3 Write the answers using decimals.

   a 75c + 75c   b 99c + 99c   c 205c − 6c

   d 205c − 66c   e 30c + 40c + 50c   f 130c + 140c + 150c

Try this

Choose two amounts that round to $3, but when added, the sum does NOT round to $6.

Write two more solutions.

Think like a mathematician

People sometimes think that $1.5 means $1 and 5 cents. To avoid confusion, use two numbers after the decimal point. $1.5 means $1.50 which is $1 and 50c.

11b Fractions and decimals

Explore

1 whole											

$\frac{1}{2}$	$\frac{1}{2}$

$\frac{1}{3}$	$\frac{1}{3}$	$\frac{1}{3}$

$\frac{1}{4}$	$\frac{1}{4}$	$\frac{1}{4}$	$\frac{1}{4}$

$\frac{1}{5}$	$\frac{1}{5}$	$\frac{1}{5}$	$\frac{1}{5}$	$\frac{1}{5}$

$\frac{1}{6}$	$\frac{1}{6}$	$\frac{1}{6}$	$\frac{1}{6}$	$\frac{1}{6}$	$\frac{1}{6}$

$\frac{1}{8}$	$\frac{1}{8}$	$\frac{1}{8}$	$\frac{1}{8}$	$\frac{1}{8}$	$\frac{1}{8}$	$\frac{1}{8}$	$\frac{1}{8}$

$\frac{1}{10}$	$\frac{1}{10}$	$\frac{1}{10}$	$\frac{1}{10}$	$\frac{1}{10}$	$\frac{1}{10}$	$\frac{1}{10}$	$\frac{1}{10}$	$\frac{1}{10}$	$\frac{1}{10}$

$\frac{1}{12}$	$\frac{1}{12}$	$\frac{1}{12}$	$\frac{1}{12}$	$\frac{1}{12}$	$\frac{1}{12}$	$\frac{1}{12}$	$\frac{1}{12}$	$\frac{1}{12}$	$\frac{1}{12}$	$\frac{1}{12}$	$\frac{1}{12}$

What is the same and what is different about each row?

Are there any rows missing? What would they look like?

What would the row for $\frac{1}{20}$ look like?

What about the row for $\frac{1}{100}$?

Key words

fraction
decimal
numerator
denominator
equivalent
mixed number
divide

Equivalent fractions and ordering fractions

Learn

$\frac{2}{4}$ is exactly the same as $\frac{1}{2}$. These fractions are equivalent fractions.

$\frac{3}{4}$ is greater than $\frac{8}{10}$.

Do you agree with Alec?
Look at the fraction wall. How can you use it to help decide?

Do you agree with Lia?

Practise

1 Use the fraction wall to write all the equivalent fractions to $\frac{1}{2}$.

2 Put these fractions in order from smallest to largest.

a $\frac{3}{10}, \frac{5}{10}, \frac{1}{10}, \frac{10}{10}, \frac{9}{10}$

b $\frac{1}{8}, \frac{5}{8}, \frac{3}{8}, \frac{7}{8}, \frac{4}{8}$

c $\frac{1}{5}, \frac{3}{5}, \frac{2}{5}, \frac{5}{5}, \frac{4}{5}$

d $\frac{1}{3}, \frac{1}{8}, \frac{1}{4}, \frac{1}{10}$

e $\frac{2}{3}, \frac{2}{8}, \frac{2}{4}, \frac{2}{10}$

f $\frac{3}{6}, \frac{2}{5}, \frac{5}{8}, \frac{4}{4}, \frac{1}{2}$

3 Which of these do you estimate has the most equivalent fractions on the wall?

List all the equivalent fractions. Were your estimates correct?

a $\frac{3}{4}$

b $\frac{4}{6}$

c $\frac{2}{8}$

d $\frac{1}{3}$

e $\frac{4}{12}$

Try this

There are no fractions equivalent to $\frac{5}{8}$ on the fraction wall.
Can you think of any fractions that would be exactly equivalent to $\frac{5}{8}$?
What about $\frac{5}{12}$?

Decimals and fractions

Learn

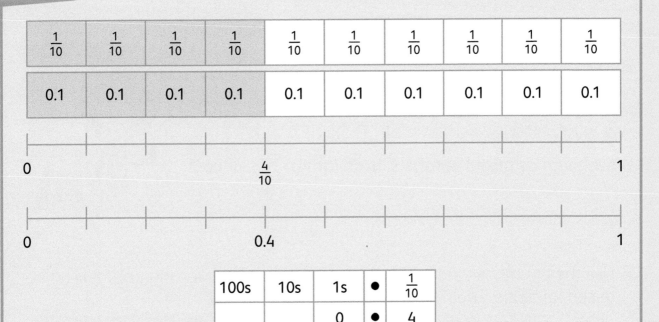

All these diagrams show different ways of representing 0.4 or $\frac{4}{10}$.

What would they look like for 0.3 or $\frac{5}{10}$?

Practise

1 Write these fractions as decimals. The first one has been done for you.

a $\frac{3}{10}$ = 0.3   b $\frac{9}{10}$ c $\frac{5}{10}$

d $\frac{1}{10}$ e $\frac{7}{10}$

2 Put these fractions and decimals in order from smallest to largest:

a $\frac{1}{4}$, 0.2, $\frac{1}{10}$, 0.3, $\frac{4}{8}$ b 0.7, $\frac{7}{8}$, $\frac{7}{12}$

c $\frac{1}{3}$, 0.3, $\frac{3}{4}$, $\frac{3}{8}$, $\frac{3}{6}$ d 0.8, $\frac{4}{6}$, 0.4, $\frac{2}{6}$, 0.5

Mixed numbers

Learn

1 whole	$\frac{1}{2}$	

1 whole	$\frac{1}{3}$	$\frac{1}{3}$

1 whole	1 whole	$\frac{1}{5}$	$\frac{1}{5}$

> A mixed number is a whole number and a fraction, such as $1\frac{1}{2}$.

Write them as mixed numbers, from largest to smallest.

Practise

1 Use the bar model and number line to convert the following decimals and mixed numbers. The first one has been done for you.

$\frac{1}{4}$	$\frac{1}{4}$	$\frac{1}{4}$	$\frac{1}{4}$	$\frac{1}{4}$	$\frac{1}{4}$	$\frac{1}{4}$	$\frac{1}{4}$

```
0     0.25    0.5    0.75    1    1.25    1.5    1.75    2
```

a $\frac{1}{4}$ = 0.25 b $\frac{3}{4}$ c $1\frac{1}{4}$ d $\frac{7}{4}$ e $\frac{9}{4}$ f 2.25   g 4.75   h 13.25

2 Write the mixed number for each arrow.

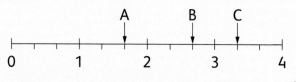

3 Write these in order; start with the largest.

a $4\frac{1}{10}$, 5.5, $4\frac{1}{2}$, $5\frac{4}{8}$, 5.0

b 5.1, $15\frac{1}{5}$, $11\frac{5}{10}$, 10.5, $11\frac{1}{10}$

c 50.5, $5\frac{1}{5}$, $15\frac{5}{10}$, 51.1, $15\frac{2}{6}$

Try this

Write these fractions as mixed numbers.

a $\frac{15}{10}$ b $\frac{15}{8}$ c $\frac{15}{6}$

d $\frac{15}{5}$ e $\frac{15}{3}$ f $\frac{15}{2}$

Fractions and division

Learn

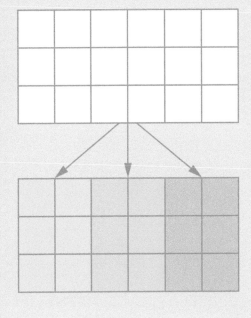

This diagram shows how you can find $\frac{1}{3}$ of a number by dividing it by 3.

Describe to a partner how Lia's method works.

$18 \div 3 = 6$

$\frac{1}{3}$ of 18 is 6

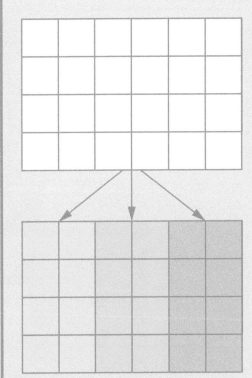

Give a division and a fraction statement for this diagram.

Try this

How many fractions of 100 have no remainder?

Practise

1 Write the answers. The first one has been done for you.

   a $\frac{1}{3}$ of 12 $12 \div 3 = 4$, $\frac{1}{3}$ of 12 = 4

   b $\frac{1}{4}$ of 12   c $\frac{1}{5}$ of 25   d $\frac{1}{5}$ of 55

2 There are 36 children in a class.

   The children named their favourite sports.

   $\frac{1}{4}$ like soccer $\frac{1}{3}$ like tennis

   $\frac{1}{6}$ like swimming $\frac{1}{9}$ like basketball

   The rest of the children like athletics.

   How many children like each sport?

3

I have shaded $\frac{1}{4}$ of this shape, because I shaded exactly 4 squares.

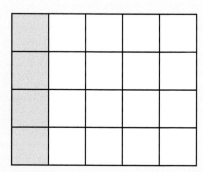

Discuss why Alec is wrong, and draw a diagram that shows the correct answer.

Try this

Look at the diagram.

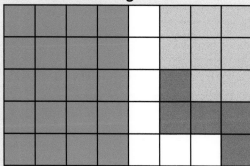

a Which colour shows $\frac{1}{2}$ of 40?

b Which colour shows $\frac{1}{5}$ of 40?

c Which colour shows $\frac{1}{8}$ of 40?

d What fraction does the other colour show?

11c **Addition and subtraction**

Explore

This is $\frac{1}{3}$ of a class. What fraction is not shown?

How many children are there in the class?

Learn

These number lines show how to find numbers that sum to 100.

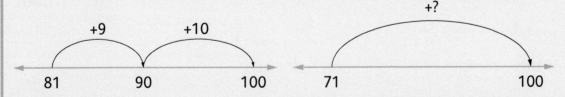

1 What method could you use to find the missing numbers for:

a 81 + ? = 100   b 71 + ? = 100   c 61 + ? = 100

2 Copy and complete the missing numbers.

a ☐ + 54 = 100   ☐ + 53 = 100   ☐ + 51 = 100

b 100 − ☐ = 44   100 − ☐ = 43   100 − ☐ = 41

3 If 75 + 25 = 100, then 750 + ☐ = 1 000?

Number bonds

4 What addition calculations would go with these diagrams?

$$\frac{1}{5} + \frac{1}{5} + \frac{1}{5} + \frac{1}{5} + \frac{1}{5} = 1$$

$$\boxed{\frac{1}{5}\ \frac{1}{5}\ \frac{1}{5}} + \boxed{\frac{1}{5}\ \frac{1}{5}} = 1$$

$$\boxed{\frac{1}{5}} + \boxed{\frac{1}{5}\ \frac{1}{5}\ \frac{1}{5}\ \frac{1}{5}} = 1$$

Practise

1 Copy and complete these calculations.

10 + ☐ + 40 = 100	120 + ☐ + 30 = 200	220 + ☐ + 130 = 400
10 + ☐ + 40 = 1 000	120 + ☐ + 30 = 1 000	220 + ☐ + 130 = 1 000

2 Copy and complete these calculations.

$\frac{1}{3} + \boxed{} = 1$ $\frac{2}{3} + \boxed{} = 1$ $\boxed{} + \frac{5}{8} = 1$ $1 = \boxed{} + \frac{7}{10}$

$\frac{1}{6} + \boxed{} = 1$ $\frac{2}{6} + \boxed{} = 1$ $\boxed{} + \frac{2}{8} = 1$ $1 = \frac{6}{10} + \boxed{}$

$\frac{1}{10} + \boxed{} = 1$ $0.2 + \boxed{} = 1$ $\boxed{} + \frac{7}{8} = 1$ $1 = \boxed{} + 0.5$

3 Use this table to answer the question below.

Class	Number of children
Class 1	24
Class 2	30
Class 3	32
Class 4	36

In Class 1, $\frac{1}{3}$ like pizza.

In Class 2, $\frac{1}{5}$ like pizza.

In Class 3, $\frac{1}{8}$ like pizza

In Class 4, $\frac{1}{6}$ like pizza.

What fraction of children in each class do not like pizza? How many children in total like pizza?

Try this

Write the answers:

$\frac{2}{3}$ of 24, $\frac{4}{5}$ of 30, $\frac{7}{8}$ of 32, and $\frac{5}{6}$ of 36.

Find the difference and subtraction

Learn

Look at these different ways of thinking about 301 − 294.

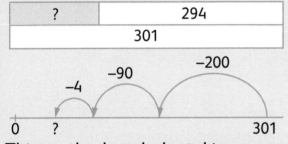

This method works by taking away 200, then taking away 90, then taking away 4.

How does this method work?

Do they come up with the same answer? Which method would you choose? Explain why.

Practise

1 Here are the heights of some trees.

What is the difference in height between:

a the orange and maple?

b the willow and the fir?

c the maple and the apple?

Name of tree	Height
maple	2.05 m
willow	303 cm
fir	2.95 m
oak	503 cm
apple	1.96 m
orange	397 cm

2 Estimate which trees have a difference nearest to:

a 100 cm   b 200 cm   c 300 cm.

Now check how close the differences are to those estimations.

3 A gardener trims 8 cm from the top of each tree. How tall are they now?

Self-check

A Number and the number system

1 Write these amounts as cents. Then write the amounts in order from smallest to largest.

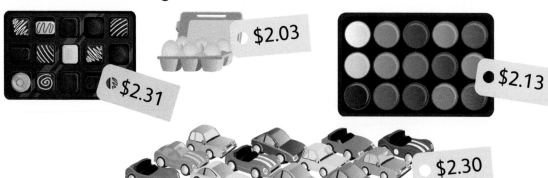

$2.03

$2.31

$2.13

$2.30

2 Write these amounts as decimals: 151c, 105c, 115c, 150c, 101c

3 Write these amounts in order, from smallest to largest: $7.50, 75c, 705c, 751c, $7.01, $0.71

B Fractions and decimals

1 Write three fractions that are equivalent to $\frac{1}{3}$.

2 Put these fractions in order from smallest to largest: $\frac{1}{5}, \frac{1}{3}, \frac{1}{8}, \frac{1}{4}, \frac{1}{2}$

3 Write $3\frac{1}{10}$ as a decimal.

4 What is $\frac{1}{5}$ of 55?

C Addition and subtraction

1 Copy and complete these calculations.

   a $\frac{4}{6}$ + ? = 1   b 10 + ? + 80 = 100

   c 201 − 8 = ?   d 501 − 494 = ?

2 Some of these calculations have errors. Use a checking method to find out which ones are incorrect.

   a 20 + 40 + 30 = 100   b 21 + 99 = 120

   c 702 − 9 = 692   d 750 + 350 = 1 000

   Discuss the method you used with a partner. Can you think of any other checking methods?

12a The metric system

Explore

What would happen if you poured the same amount of water into the tall glass and the short glass?

How many tall glasses do you estimate it would take to fill the bath?

How could you estimate how many baths of water it would take to fill the swimming pool?

Key words

litre
millilitre
capacity
measure
liquid

Reading scales

Learn

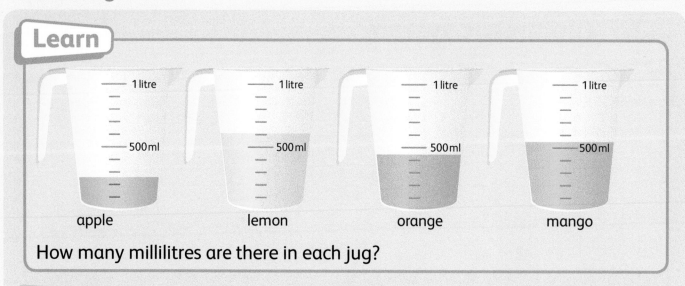

apple   lemon   orange   mango

How many millilitres are there in each jug?

Practise

1 Which jugs add together to make 1 litre? The first one has been done for you.

Jug a and Jug j make 1 litre. 300 ml + 700 ml = 1 litre

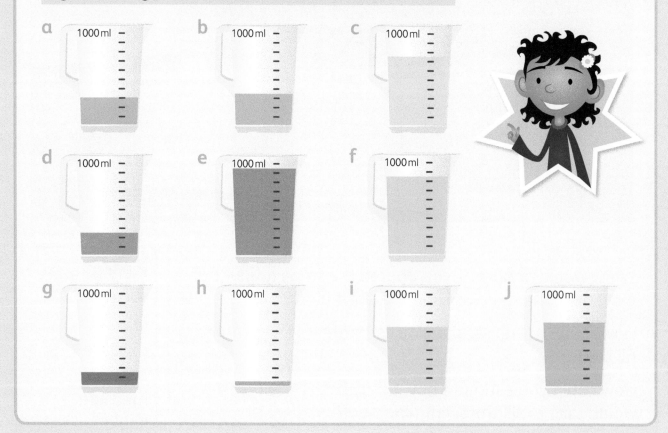

Practise

2 Estimate how much is in each jug.

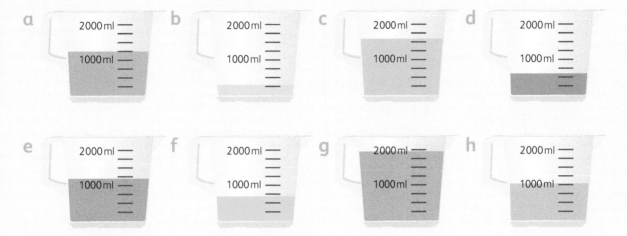

3 Look at the juice in the 'Learn' panel.

225 ml of water is added to each jug.

Then the apple and the lemon are poured into one big jug.

And the mango and orange are poured into a different jug.

Which jug has the most juice now?

Try this

Collect an empty water container. Measure how much it weighs.

Now add 100 ml of water and weigh it again.

Repeat, adding 100 ml of water until the container is nearly full.

What do you notice about how the weight changes every time you add 100 ml?

Think like a mathematician

Look closely at the divisions on the scale.

Work out what each mark stands for, and use that to help you estimate more accurately.

Converting measures

Learn

A recipe says I need to use $2\frac{1}{4}\ell$ of water. How can I measure that using a 1ℓ jug?

Practise

1   Match the equal measurements. Write the matching pairs of equivalents in your book. The first one has been done for you.

$1\frac{1}{4}\ell = 1\,250\,ml$

$1\frac{1}{4}\ell$	$2\,750\,ml$
$2\frac{3}{4}\ell$	$7\,250\,ml$
$2\frac{1}{2}\ell$	$2\,500\,ml$
$4\frac{1}{2}\ell$	$4\,500\,ml$
$5\frac{1}{2}\ell$	$7\,500\,ml$
6ℓ	$1\,250\,ml$
$7\frac{1}{2}\ell$	$5\,500\,ml$
$7\frac{1}{4}\ell$	$6\,000\,ml$

2   Convert these measures. The first one has been done for you.

a $\frac{1}{2}kg = 500\,g$ b $\frac{3}{4}kg = ?\,g$ c $1\frac{3}{4}kg = ?\,g$

d $?\,kg = 2\,750\,g$ e $\frac{1}{2}m = ?\,cm$ f $\frac{3}{4}m = ?\,cm$

g $1\frac{1}{4}m = ?\,cm$ h $?\,m = 225\,cm$

12b Area and perimeter

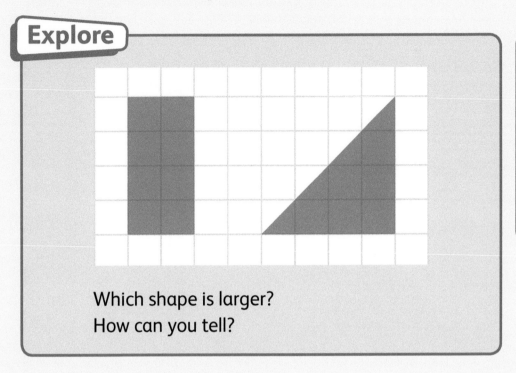

Which shape is larger?
How can you tell?

Key words

area
perimeter
length
width
half

Counting half squares

Learn

When you find the area, sometimes a shape only covers half of a square.
You can add the two halves together to be equal to a whole square.

Look at this diagram.

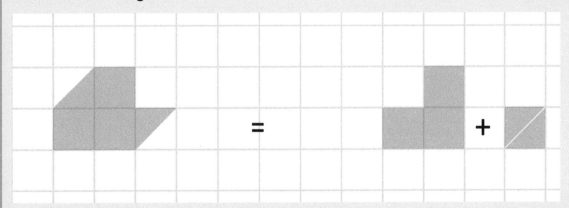

What is the area of the shape on the left?

Practise

1 Find the area of each shape. The first one has been done for you.

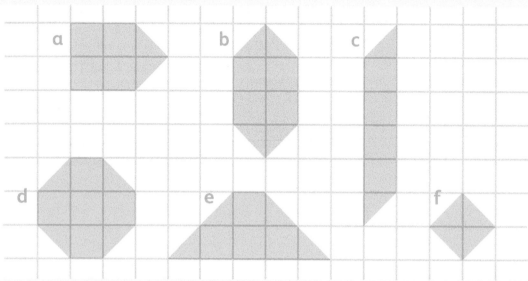

a $1 + 1 + 1 + 1 + \frac{1}{2}$ and $\frac{1}{2} = 5$

2 On squared paper, draw 8 different shapes that have an area equal to this orange rectangle.

Make sure each shape includes some half-squares.

3 Look at these squares.

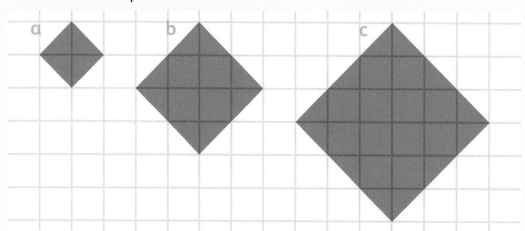

Predict the area of each. Then check your answers by counting the squares to see if you were correct.

12c Time

Explore

Can you find your birthday? Does anyone in the class have a birthday in the same week as you?

Which month has the most birthdays?

Find three more dates that are important to you.

January

Su	Mo	Tu	We	Th	Fr	Sa
1	2	3	4	5	6	7
8	9	10	11	12	13	14
15	16	17	18	19	20	21
22	23	24	25	26	27	28
29	30	31				

February

Su	Mo	Tu	We	Th	Fr	Sa
			1	2	3	4
5	6	7	8	9	10	11
12	13	14	15	16	17	18
19	20	21	22	23	24	25
26	27	28				

March

Su	Mo	Tu	We	Th	Fr	Sa
			1	2	3	4
5	6	7	8	9	10	11
12	13	14	15	16	17	18
19	20	21	22	23	24	25
26	27	28	29	30	31	

April

Su	Mo	Tu	We	Th	Fr	Sa
						1
2	3	4	5	6	7	8
9	10	11	12	13	14	15
16	17	18	19	20	21	22
23	24	25	26	27	28	29
30						

May

Su	Mo	Tu	We	Th	Fr	Sa
	1	2	3	4	5	6
7	8	9	10	11	12	13
14	15	16	17	18	19	20
21	22	23	24	25	26	27
28	29	30	31			

June

Su	Mo	Tu	We	Th	Fr	Sa
				1	2	3
4	5	6	7	8	9	10
11	12	13	14	15	16	17
18	19	20	21	22	23	24
25	26	27	28	29	30	

Juy

Su	Mo	Tu	We	Th	Fr	Sa
						1
2	3	4	5	6	7	8
9	10	11	12	13	14	15
16	17	18	19	20	21	22
23	24	25	26	27	28	29
30	31					

August

Su	Mo	Tu	We	Th	Fr	Sa
		1	2	3	4	5
6	7	8	9	10	11	12
13	14	15	16	17	18	19
20	21	22	23	24	25	26
27	28	29	30	31		

September

Su	Mo	Tu	We	Th	Fr	Sa
					1	2
3	4	5	6	7	8	9
10	11	12	13	14	15	16
17	18	19	20	21	22	23
24	25	26	27	28	29	30

October

Su	Mo	Tu	We	Th	Fr	Sa
1	2	3	4	5	6	7
8	9	10	11	12	13	14
15	16	17	18	19	20	21
22	23	24	25	26	27	28
29	30	31				

November

Su	Mo	Tu	We	Th	Fr	Sa
			1	2	3	4
5	6	7	8	9	10	11
12	13	14	15	16	17	18
19	20	21	22	23	24	25
26	27	28	29	30		

December

Su	Mo	Tu	We	Th	Fr	Sa
					1	2
3	4	5	6	7	8	9
10	11	12	13	14	15	16
17	18	19	20	21	22	23
24	25	26	27	28	29	30
31						

Problem solving about calendars

Learn

What is the date and day on which Alec says this?

It is six days until my birthday party! I am very excited.

KEY	
☆	Cricket match
●	Lia's party
▲	Alec's party
▨	School holiday

JUNE						
Sun	Mon	Tues	Weds	Thurs	Fri	Sat
				1	2	3 ☆
4	5 ▲	6 ☆	7	8	9 ●	10
11	12	13	14	15 ☆	16	17
18	19	20	21	22	23	24
25	26	27 ☆	28	29	30	

Practise

1 Write the dates of all the cricket matches, the holidays, and both birthday parties. The first one has been done for you. Cricket match on Tuesday 6 June.

2 a How many days are there between Alec's party and Lia's party?

b What is the date two weeks after Lia's party?

c How long is the longest gap between cricket matches?

3 a Lia's actual birthday is a fortnight (two weeks) before her party. What is the date of her birthday?

b The cricket final is ten days after the last match in June. What is the date of the final?

Try this

Look at the calendar in the 'Learn' panel. Work out on which day of the week Alec's birthday will fall in the coming year.

⟳ 12d Problem solving

Explore

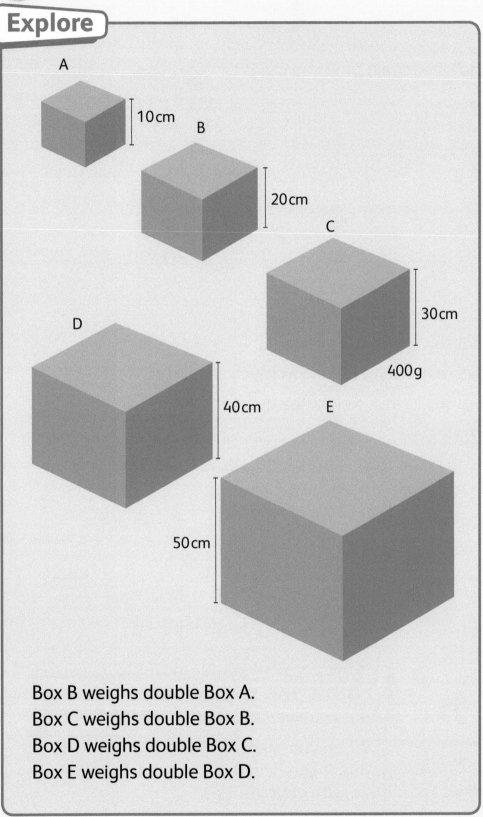

A

10 cm

B

20 cm

C

30 cm

400 g

D

40 cm

E

50 cm

Key words ⟳
solve
solution
reason
explain
measure
length
weight
capacity

Box B weighs double Box A.
Box C weighs double Box B.
Box D weighs double Box C.
Box E weighs double Box D.

Explaining reasoning

Learn

Explain two ways that Alec could prove he is right.

> I know that a stack of four Box B boxes weighs the same as one Box D.

Practise

1 Design five different stacks that are 1 m tall.

Show the stack using a diagram. Label how much each stack weighs.

2 Design five different stacks that weigh exactly 1 kg.

Label how tall each stack is.

3 Predict which of each pair would be taller, and which would be heavier.

 a 10 of Box A or 2 of Box D

 b 5 of Box A or 3 of Box C

 c 5 of Box B or 2 of Box C

 d 10 of Box B or 2 of Box D.

Try this

Design a stack that weighs exactly 3 kg and is exactly 140 cm tall.

Think like a mathematician

When you are working on problems like this, it can help to draw a quick diagram to go with your jottings.

Self-check

A The metric system
Copy and complete the missing information.

1 ☐ ml = $\frac{1}{2}$ litre

2 4 500 ml = ☐ litre

3 $\frac{1}{2}$ m + $\frac{1}{4}$ m = ☐ cm

B Area and perimeter

1 Draw a shape with an area of $2\frac{1}{2}$ squares.

2 Draw a shape with an area of 5 squares that is not a rectangle.

3 Copy these rectangles and write their areas and perimeters:

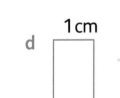

C Time

1 What is the date one week before the 8th May?

2 Which month has the fewest days?

3 How many days are in April?

4 What is the date two weeks after the 20th of December?

Unit 13 Number and problem solving

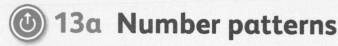 13a Number patterns

Explore

Pattern 1

Pattern 2

Pattern 3

Pattern 4

Can you spot how the patterns change?

Work out the next two shapes, and the next two colours, in these patterns.

Work out the colour and shape of the 20th and 30th shape in each pattern.

Do you have to draw all of the shapes, or can you use number patterns and times tables to help?

Think like a mathematician

Use reasoning to work out the 100th shape in the patterns in the 'Explore' panel.

Key words

pattern
multiple
odd
even
increase
decrease

Reasoning about patterns

Learn

How can you tell which of these will have zero and which will not?

800, 700, 600, 500, …

30, 27, 24, 21, …

55, 50, 45, 40, 35, …

48, 44, 40, 36, …

49, 45, 41, 37, …

I can tell that these sequences will have zero in them, because I recognise the times tables.

Practise

1 Which of these sequences will have zero in them?

   a 25, 30, 35, 40, …   b 95, 90, 85, 80 …

   c 41, 36, 31, 25, …   d 86, 88, 90, 92, …

   e 88, 86, 84, 82, …   f 42, 39, 36, 33, …

   g 28, 25, 22, …   h 321, 311, 301, …

   i 550, 540, 530, …

2 Work out the next three numbers in each sequence. The first one has been done for you.

   a 11, 31, 51, 71, 91, 111, 131   b 191, 171, 151, ?, ?, ?

   c 990, 890, 790, ?, ?, ?   d 991, 891, 791, ?, ?, ?

   e 103, 106, 109, ?, ?, ?   f 204, 208, 212, ?, ?, ?

   g 105, 109, 113, ?, ?, ?   h 108, 105, 102, ?, ?, ?

Adding multiples of 10 and 100, and reasoning about odd and even numbers

Learn

When you add 100 to a number, only the hundreds digit changes.

When you subtract 10 from a number, only the tens digit changes.

345 + 100   345 − 10

885 + 100   885 − 10

These examples suggest the statements are always true.

Can you think of any calculations that disprove the statements?

Practise

1 Copy and complete these calculations. The first one has been done for you.

a
155 + 10 = 165

155 + 20 = ☐

155 + 40 = ☐

155 + 80 = ☐

b
155 + 100 = ☐

155 + 200 = ☐

155 + 400 = ☐

155 + 800 = ☐

c
☐ = 1 555 + 1 000

☐ = 1 555 + 2 000

☐ = 1 555 + 4 000

☐ = 1 555 + 8 000

2 Calculate the mystery number.

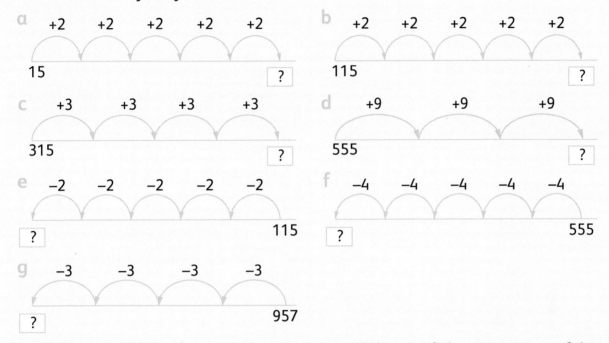

a
+2 +2 +2 +2 +2
15   ?

b
+2 +2 +2 +2 +2
115   ?

c
+3   +3   +3   +3
315   ?

d
+9   +9   +9
555   ?

e
−2 −2 −2 −2 −2
?   115

f
−4   −4   −4   −4   −4
?   555

g
−3   −3   −3   −3
?   957

3 Find three examples for each statement, and decide if they are true or false.

Make sure that your examples use three-digit, two-digit and one-digit numbers.

If you add three odd numbers together, you get an odd answer.

If you add five even numbers together, you get an odd answer.

Try this

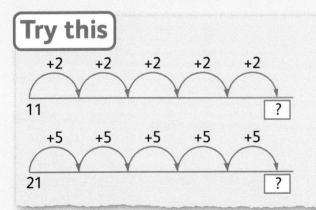

+2 +2 +2 +2 +2
11   ?

+5 +5 +5 +5 +5
21   ?

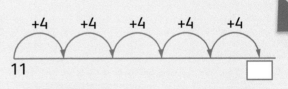

+4   +4   +4   +4   +4
11   ☐

Do you have to work out all the jumps to decide if the missing number will be odd or even?

13b **Multiplication and division**

Explore

How many yellow and how many blue squares are there in the next pattern?

Times tables and division facts

Learn

Attraction	Adult price	Child price
Cinema	$9	$6
Fairground	$5	$3
Boat-trip	$4	$2

A group of adults spent $45 going to the fairground. How many adults were there?

I check my divisions by using the inverse.

$$45 \div 5 = 9$$

This must be right because $5 \times 9 = 45$.

Practise

1 Which is more expensive? The first one has been done for you.

  a Five adults to go to the fairground, or 8 children?

> Adults: $5 × 5 = $25   Children: $3 × 8 = $24.
> It is more expensive for the five adults to go.

  b Nine adults to go on the boat trip, or 5 children?

  c Six adults to go to the cinema, or 8 children?

  d Five children to go to the fairground, or 3 adults?

2 a Adults spent $24 going on a boat-trip, then they all went to the fairground. How much did they spend altogether?

  b Children spent $42 going to the cinema, then they all went to the fairground. How much did they spend altogether?

Try this

The same number of adults and children spent $48 going on a boat trip.

How many of each were there?

Learn

A Multiply and divide three-digit numbers by 10 and 100

THs	Hs	Ts	Us
	1	2	4
1	2	4	0

124 × 10 = ?   ? × 10 = 3 450

224 × 10 = ?   ? × 10 = 4 550

324 × 10 = ?   ? × 10 = 5 550

24 × 100 = ?

? × 100 = 3 400

5 400 ÷ 100 = ?

B Doubling

I am playing a doubling game. I choose a starting number between 1 and 20. I double it, then add one. I double and add one. I keep going, until I go past 100.

Start with the number 7.

How many steps does it take to go past 100?

Practise

1 Copy and complete these doubles. The first one has been done for you.

a Double 15 = 30
  Double 14
  Double 16

b Double 25
  Double 24
  Double 26

c Double 150
  Double 140
  Double 160

d Double ? = 500
  Double ? = 480
  Double ? = 460

2 Play Lia's 'double and add one' game.

Use these starting numbers. What is the first number you reach past 100 for each starting number?

a 5   b 10   c 12   d 20

3 Test Alec's theory, by choosing different starting numbers between 1 and 20.

Do you agree with him?

What if you were allowed to choose any starting number?

> It is impossible to reach exactly 100 when playing Lia's game.

4 You can use doubling to check multiplicatons.

Look how Sanjay checks his calculation.

3 × 8 = 24
3 × 4 = 12,
double 12 = 24

Can you explain how Sanjays's checking strategy works?

Use this technique to check these:

a 6 × 8 = 48

b 12 × 5 = 60

Try this

Here is Alec's version of the game: I choose a multiple of 10. I double it and add 10. I keep going until I go past 1000.

Is it possible to reach 1000 playing his game?

Rounding up or down after division with remainders

Learn

Fence panels come in packs of 4.

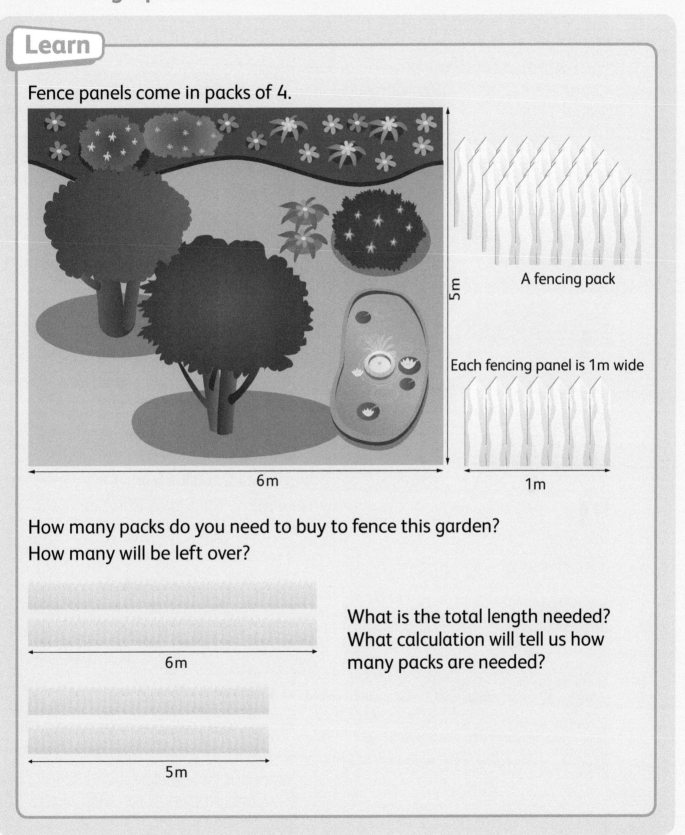

A fencing pack

Each fencing panel is 1m wide

6m

1m

5m

How many packs do you need to buy to fence this garden?
How many will be left over?

6m

5m

What is the total length needed?
What calculation will tell us how many packs are needed?

Practise

1 Predict which of these will have an answer greater than 10. Which will have a remainder? Check using multiplication or division. The first one has been done for you.

    a $72 \div 5$ **Predict:** answer > 10, because 10×5 is already 50, and $72 > 50$.
                 Predict: it will have a remainder as a number ending in 2 is not
                 a multiple of 5.
                 Check: $72 \div 5 = 14$ remainder 2. Both the predictions were correct.

    b $72 \div 10$ c $72 \div 6$ d $72 \div 2$ e $72 \div 3$ f $72 \div 11$

2 Work out how many packs you will need to buy for each garden. The first one has been done for you.

    a

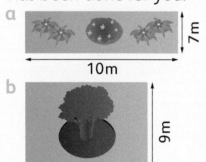

10 m by 7 m → $10\ m \times 2 = 20\ m$ and $7\ m \times 2 = 14\ m$, $20\ m + 14\ m = 34\ m$.
$34 \div 4 = 8$ remainder 2. But 8 packs are not enough.
$9 \times 4 = 36$. So you will need 9 packs, and have 2 panels left over.

    b

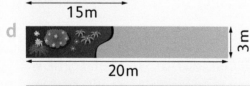

3 The head teacher has to decide on the number of tables to use for the lunch hall to seat 66 children.

How many full tables will there be if there are tables for:

    a 3 people   b 5 people   c 6 people

    d 9 people   e 10 people.

Will anyone have to sit on their own for any of these options?

    c

    d

    e

Try this

Fence panels in packs of 4 cost $5.
In packs of 5 they cost $6.
Work out the cheapest way to buy fencing panels for each of the gardens in Question 2.

Proportion

Learn

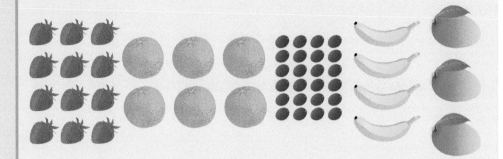

Recipe for fruit salad
(Serves 2)
12 strawberries
6 oranges
24 grapes
4 bananas
3 mangoes

This recipe makes enough fruit salad for two people.

How much of each fruit would you need for six people?

What diagrams would help solve this problem?
Which of the calculations can you do mentally, and which need a written method?

Practise

1 Calculate the number of each fruit you would need for eight people.

2 How much would you use if you wanted to make a fruit salad for three people? Explain your reasons to a partner.

3 For a party, there were 36 bananas in total.

   How many people would that recipe serve?

   Write the recipe for this fruit salad.

Try this

You want to make a fruit salad for 11 people. How many of each fruit would you need to buy?
Would you have any left over at the end?

Proportion problems

Learn

The class make some letters to display around the school.
Medium-sized letters are two times as wide and two times as tall as the small letters.
Large letters are three times as wide and tall as the small letters.

small-size letters

A ↕ 5 cm
↔
4 cm

Practise

1 The class make a sign saying: 'WELCOME'.

  Work out how tall and wide the signs will be. The first one has been done for you.

  a They use small lettering. The height of the sign = 5 cm.

     The width → 7 letters in WELCOME × 4 cm → 28 cm.

  b They use medium lettering.

2 The class make a sign for everyone's name.

  Write these name signs in order from shortest to widest.

Name	Letter size
ALEC	medium
LIA	large
FELIX	medium
MAYA	large
ORLANDO	medium
ACE	medium

3 There are also extra-large letters. These are nine times as wide as the small letters.
  Work out how wide the signs would be for each name using the extra-large letters.

Try this

Write your own sentence and calculate how much wider it would be in medium letters than small letters.

Ratio problems

Learn

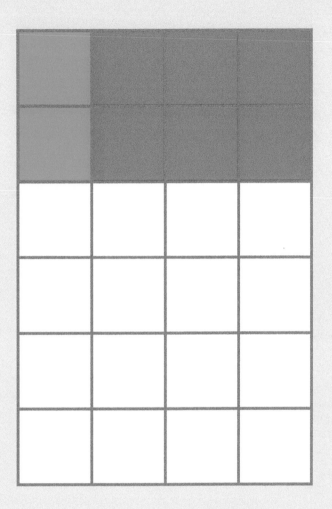

Lia wants to make a design with blue and red squares.
She colours one blue square, then three red squares.
Then she colours one more blue, and three more red.
She keeps going until she has filled the grid.
How many blue squares will she have in total?

Practise

1 Use these grids to make a pattern of one red, then two blue counters.

Keep a record of how many blue and how many red you need for each diagram.

Grid A   Grid B   Grid C

Try this

This recipe makes enough juice for 4 people to drink.

Mixed fruit juice
2 bananas
5 apples
10 strawberries

Write the recipe to make enough for:

a 12 people

b 20 people

c 6 people.

13c Problem solving

Explore

How could you quickly make 100 using this simple calculator?

Can you think of more than one way?

Think like a mathematician

You will have to think about working out the calculations in stages.

5 − 2 × 5 and 5 × 5 − 2

Mathematicians expect these to have different answers. Can you explain why?

Multiplication and division puzzles

Practise

1 Using the simple calculator in the 'Explore' panel, how could you make these numbers? Use the fewest number of presses. The first one has been done for you.

   a 20 $5 \times 2 \times 2$

   b 13   c 23   d 15

   e 30   f 46   g 125

2 If you work from left to right, these digit cards will give you 10:

   | 5 | × 4 | ÷ 2 |

   Use two or more digit cards to make the target answers.

   | × 4 | × 10 | ÷ 5 | ÷ 2 |

   | 1 | 3 | 5 | 20 |

Target
200
60
100
24
3

3 Look at these calculations:

   a 20×5 b 35×2 c 61×8

   d $1\,300 \times 2$ e $550 \div 10$ f 75×100

   Discuss with a partner the different methods you would use to solve them.

   Then solve them together, showing your workings.

Try this

Using the simple calculator, see if you can make all the numbers from 1 to 20.

Self-check

A Number patterns

1 Copy and complete the sequences:

a 25, 50, ☐, 100, ☐, 150

b 250, 230, ☐, 190, ☐, ☐

c ☐, ☐, ☐, 96, 93, 90

d 1, ☐, 41, ☐, 81, ☐

2 Write 10 more, 100 more and 1 000 more than each number:

a 1 234

b 4 321

c 4 343

d 1 212

B Multiplication and division

1 4 × 9 = ?

2 8 × 3 = ?

3 6 × 8 = ?

4 What is double 33?

5 What number doubled is 52?

6 What is the remainder for 89 ÷ 4?

7 If you need 4 eggs to make one cake, how many eggs do you need to make 5 cakes?

14a Classifying shapes

Explore

Key words

prism
pyramid
cuboid
net
vertices
faces
edges

What 3-D shapes can you name in this environment?

Are any of the same shapes in your school or classroom?

What is the most common shape?

Properties of 3-D shapes

Learn

Which one is a prism, and which is a pyramid? How can you tell?

If you can't remember the difference between a prism and a pyramid, then use the dictionary to remind yourself.

Which has the most edges, vertices or faces?

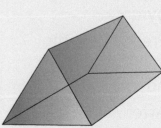

Practise

1 Here are the bases for five different pyramids.

 a 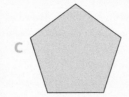 b 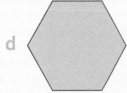 c 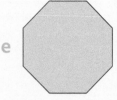 d 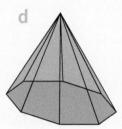 e

Work out how many vertices, faces and edges each pyramid would have.

2 Which of these has an even number of faces?

How do you know?

a 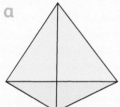 b 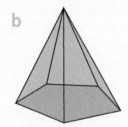 c 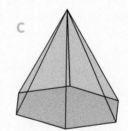 d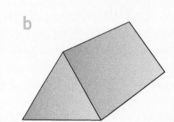

Which has an odd number of vertices?

3 Explain the similarities and differences for these two shapes. Compare the faces, vertices and edges. Add any extra observations.

a 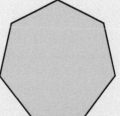 b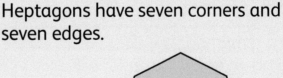

Try this

Sketch or use construction materials to make a heptagonal-based pyramid.

Predict how many vertices, faces and edges it will have before you make it.

After making it, check to see if you were right.

Think like a mathematician

Heptagons have seven corners and seven edges.

Recognising quadrilaterals

Learn

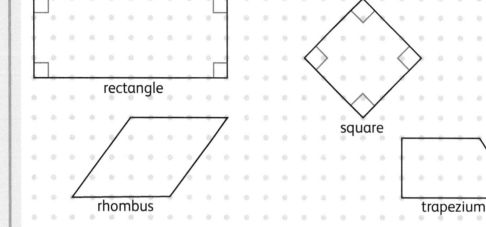

rectangle

square

irregular quadrilateral

rhombus

trapezium

A quadrilateral is a 2-D shape with four straight sides.

A rectangle is a quadrilateral with four right angles.

A rhombus is a quadrilateral with four equal sides.

True or false: a square is both a rhombus and a rectangle?

Think like a mathematician

Check your own rhombus shapes by measuring the sides. They should all be the same length.

Try this

Use 3-D construction materials to make a solid shape that has at least one rhombus-shaped face.

Now try to make a prism or a pyramid that has a kite as a face.

Practise

1 Make these shapes on a pinboard or draw them on dotty paper.

1 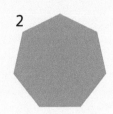   2    3    4

5 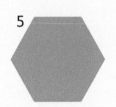   6    7    8

9    10

2 Write the number of every shape that is:

a a quadrilateral

b a rectangle

c a rhombus

d a square

e a hexagon

f a heptagon.

Be careful! The same shape may be in more than one group.

3 Look at the shapes in question 1.

Sort them into shapes that have:

a one line of symmetry

b two lines of symmetry

c more than two lines of symmetry

d zero lines of symmetry.

4 On dotty paper, draw six different rhombus shapes. Include two different squares.

14b 3-D and 2-D shapes

Explore

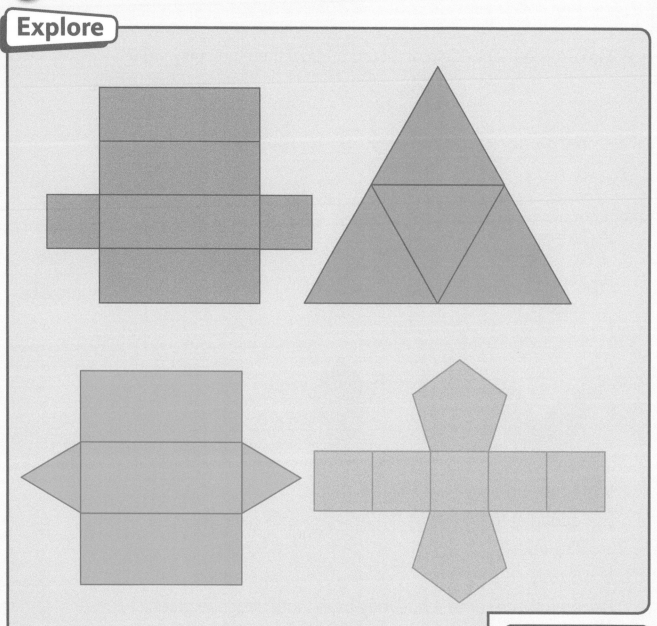

Name the 3-D shapes these nets would form.

Can you tell how many faces, vertices or edges each would have, just by looking at the net?

Key words

net
cube
cuboid
symmetrical
symmetry

Symmetry in nets and 3-D shapes

Learn

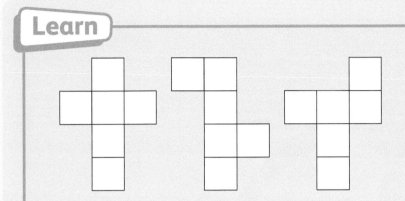

One of these nets is symmetrical. Can you see which one it is?

Where would the line of symmetry go?

Practise

1 Use construction materials to find five more nets of a cube, including one with a line of symmetry. Draw the net and show the line of symmetry.

2 Look at the net of this triangular prism. Copy it and sketch in two lines of symmetry.

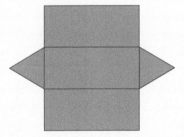

3 Draw a symmetrical net for a cuboid, and one that is not symmetrical.

Try this

Draw the nets for different pyramids.

Sketch in lines of symmetry on the diagrams.

Think like a mathematician

When drawing a net, it may help to make the 3-D shape out of construction materials, then use that shape to help draw the net.

14c **Position and movement**

Explore

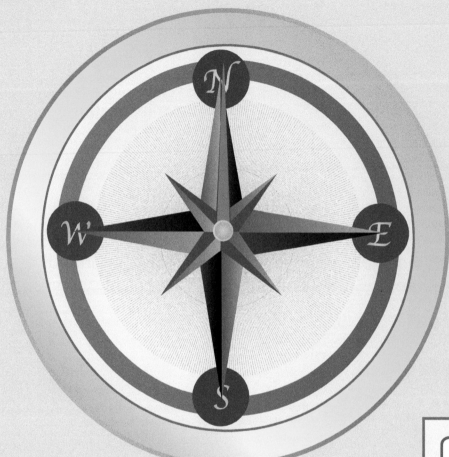

What is the name for this instrument?

What do the letters mean?

Do you know which way you are facing now?

Key words

angle

right angle

acute

obtuse

direction

turn

north

east

west

south

Think like a mathematician

Look carefully at the compass to help you solve the turning puzzles. Try turning the page if it helps.

Different kinds of angles

Learn

quarter-turn 90°

half-turn 180°

whole-turn 360°

A quarter-turn is also called a right angle.

obtuse

acute

If a turn is less than a right angle, it is called 'acute'.

If a turn is between a quarter-turn and a half-turn, it is called 'obtuse'.

Try this

Use some 2-D shapes from the classroom. Draw them and label each interior angle as either acute, obtuse or right angle.

Practise

1 Use the picture on the right to answer these questions. Which direction would the person face if he:

a turned 180 degrees?

b turned by a right angle?

c How many degrees would he have to turn to be facing east again?

2 Decide whether each angle shows a quarter-turn, an acute angle, or an obtuse angle. The first one has been done for you.

a   b   c   d   e   f   g   h

acute

3 Draw the following shapes and label the angles.

a a triangle with three acute angles

b a triangle with one obtuse angle

c a four-sided shape with two acute angles and two obtuse angles

d a hexagon with three obtuse angles and three acute angles.

Directions and turns

Learn

Start on A1.

Travel north three squares, and east for one square.

What shape do you finish on?

Describe the journey from E1 to each of the shapes in the grid. You can only travel north, south, east or west, not diagonally.

Practise

Play a game with your partner. Choose a counter each. Place it on the grid.

Choose which direction you want to move, then spin the spinner.

You move north, south, east or west as many squares as are shown on the spinner.

You cannot move off the edge of the board.

The winner is the first person to capture the other person's counter by landing on it.

Self-check

A **Classifying shapes**

1 How many vertices are there on a square-based pyramid?
2 How many vertices are there on a heptagonal prism?
3 What are the properties of a rhombus?
4 What does the word 'quadrilateral' mean?

B **3-D and 2-D shapes**

Net		Shape	
1		A	
2	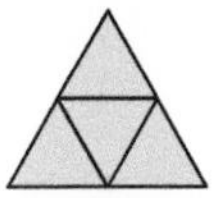	B	
3	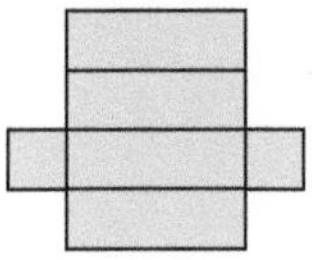	C	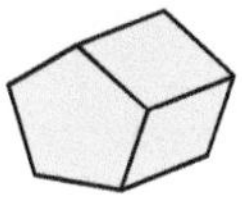
4	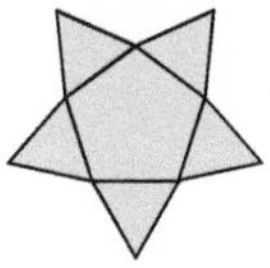	D	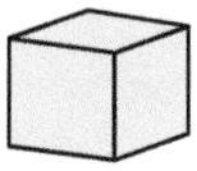
5	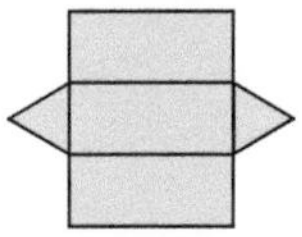	E	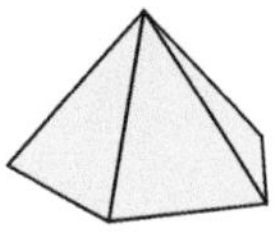
6	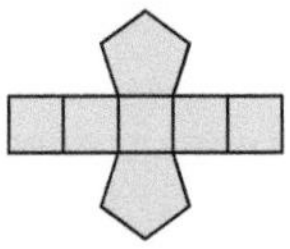	F	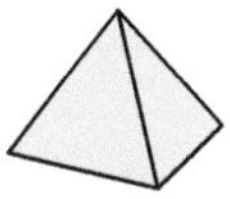

Which net matches which shape? Write the number and the correct letter.

C **Position and movement**

1 Draw an acute angle and an obtuse angle.
2 How many degrees are there in a quarter-turn?
3 Where would you be facing if you turned a half-turn from west?
4 Describe the journey from triangle to star in the grid from the 'Learn' panel on page 166.

Unit 15 Problem solving and review

15a Problem solving

Explore

Are there more or less than one hundred items in this picture?

Key words
estimate
predict
puzzle
pattern
check

Picture problems

1 Make jottings to make a good estimate of the number of items in the picture. Show how you split the problem into steps.

2 If you could carry fifty fruits in a basket, how many baskets would you need for all this fruit? Give reasons for your answer.

3 If you sold half of the fruits on one day, and then half of what was left on the following day, how many fruits would you have left?

Story problems

Look at the fruit price list:

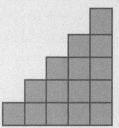

Apple – 10ᶜ   Guava – 80ᶜ

Orange – 20ᶜ   Pomegranate – 160ᶜ

Mango – 40ᶜ   Watermelon – 160ᶜ

1 Lia spends exactly $2.50 on three different fruits. What did she buy?

2 How many mangos would cost the same as:
   a two guavas   b two pomegranates   c three watermelons   d 20 apples.

3 Alec bought four different items and spent less than $4.

   Write five different combinations of fruit he could have bought.

Try this

Spend $3 on fruit. You can only buy one of each type of fruit. How many ways can you spend $3?

Calculation problems

  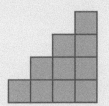

1 Count how many squares there are in each pattern.
2 How many squares would there be in the next pattern? Draw it to check.
3 Calculate the answers.

   a $1 + 2 = ?$

   b $1 + 2 + 3 = ?$

   c $1 + 2 + 3 + 4 = ?$

   d $1 + 2 + 3 + 4 + 5 = ?$

   e $1 + 2 + 3 + 4 + 5 + 6 = ?$

   Keep this pattern going until the answer to the addition passes 100. Describe and explain the pattern of odd and even answers.

Think like a mathematician

You can use cubes or counters to help you with the design of the patterns. Try using a different colour for each row.

Pattern problems

1 Give calculations for how many oranges are in each layer of the stack.

Show the total for the stack.

2 How many oranges would there be if another layer was added? Draw a diagram to help work this out.

3 An orange weighs approximately 100 g. How many layers would you need until the weight of the stack is over 5 kg?

4 What is the same and what is different about this stack compared with the stack above?

Work out how many there are in each row, and then how many there would be in a stack with five layers.

Try this

Add the numbers below together to make the totals in the cloud.

1, 3, 6, 10, 15, 21, 28, 36, 45, 55, 66, 78

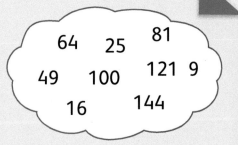

64   25   81
49   100   121 9
16   144

Mathematical dictionary

2-D shape a flat shape

3-D shape a solid shape

A

a.m. before midday

acute an angle that is less than 90 degrees

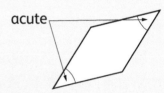

add to find a sum

addition a calculation of the sum of two numbers or things

analogue showing time by the hands of a clock or watch

angle the amount of turn between where two lines meet

area the amount of space that a flat surface or a shape covers

array a rectangular arrangement of quantities

3 × 3

B

balance to have weight evenly on one side and the other

bar chart a chart that uses bars to show the relationship between groups of information

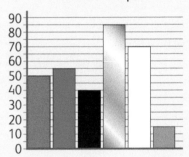

Cars in a car park

C

calculate to find the amount or number

calendar a set of pages or tables that show the days, weeks and months of a year

capacity the amount of space that a container has to hold things

Carroll diagram used to sort items according to two groups

centimetre a unit for measuring the length of something;
100 centimetres = 1 metre

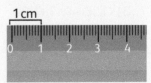

1 cm

chart information in the form of a table, graph or diagram

check make sure, do the calculation again

classify arrange according to properties

clock a device used for telling the time

composite shape a shape that can be divided into one or more basic shapes

cube a box-shaped object with six square faces

cuboid a box-shaped object with six rectangular faces

D

data information

decimal a number less than 1; decimals are shown by using a full stop, followed by tenths, hundredths, etc., example: 0.1 means one tenth

decrease get smaller

degrees a unit of measurement of angles

denominator a number in a fraction below the line, called the divisor

$\longrightarrow \dfrac{3}{4}$

diagonal a straight line which joins two opposite corners of a polygon

digit one of the written signs we use to represent the numbers 1 to 9

digital clock a clock that displays the time using digits; these clocks do not have moving hands. It can display time using either a 12-hour or 24-hour system.

direction course or path along which something or someone moves

divide to find how many times a number goes into another number

divisible when a number can be divided by another number without a remainder

division separating something into equal parts

double twice as many

E

east the direction 90 degrees clockwise from north

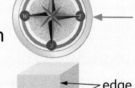

edge the side of an object

edge

equivalent the same value as

estimate to try to judge the value, size, amount, cost, speed, etc. of something without calculating it exactly

even number a number that is exactly divisible by 2

event something that happens

explain make something clear by giving reasons or details

F

faces surfaces of a solid shape

find the difference subtract one thing from another

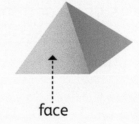

face

fraction a part of something or a part of a number

frequency how often something happens

G

gram the basic unit for measuring weight in the metric system; 1 000 grams = 1 kilogram

grid reference a letter and number to give the position of a square or other object in a grid

group to gather/collect

H

half/halve to divide by 2

height how tall a person or object is

hexagon a 2-D shape with 6 sides

horizontal level to the ground, at a right angle to the vertical

hour a unit used for measuring time; 1 hour = 60 minutes

hundred ten groups of ten

I

increase get bigger in size or number

inverse the opposite of an operation, for example subtraction is the inverse of addition

J

jottings quick or rough notes that show your working out when trying to solve a problem

K

kilogram a measurement of weight (1 000 grams)

L

length how far from one point to another

liquid a substance that flows, like water

list write items one below the other

litre a unit of measurement of volume or capacity

M

mass a measure of how much matter (material) is in an object; mass can be measured in grams and kilograms.

measure to find out the size or weight of something by using a standard tool such as a measuring tape or a measuring scale

method way to do something

metre a unit for measuring length or distance

midday the middle of the day, 12 noon

millilitre a unit for measuring volume; 1 000 millilitres = 1 litre.

millimetre a unit for measuring length; 1 000 millimetres = 1 metre.

minus take away or subtract

minute there are 60 minutes in one hour

mixed number a number that consists of a whole number and a fraction or decimal, for example: $5 \frac{3}{4}$ or 5.75

money coins or banknotes used to pay for goods and services

month there are 12 months in a year: January, February, March, April, May, June, July, August, September, October, November, December

multiple a number that can be divided equally by another number without a remainder

N

negative number numbers that are less than zero

net a pattern on paper that you can cut and fold to make a model of a 3-D shape

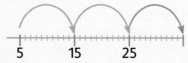

north the direction in which a compass needle points

number bonds the relationship between a number and the numbers that make it up, for example: 6 and 4 are number bonds for 10

number line a line with points which represent numbers

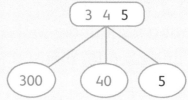

numeral a figure or symbol that represents a number

numerator the number above the line in a fraction; in the fraction $\frac{2}{5}$, 2 is the numerator $\longrightarrow \frac{2}{5}$

O

o'clock used to give the hour when telling time

obtuse an angle that is bigger than 90 degrees, but less than 180 degrees

obtuse

odd number numbers that are not exactly divisible by 2, for example: 1, 3, 5, 7

P

p.m. after 12 noon, in the afternoon

partition to break numbers up into different parts, for example you could partition the number 43 512 into 40 000 + 3 000 + 500 + 10 + 2

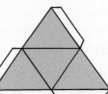

pattern something that is repeated

pentagon a 2-D shape with 5 sides

perimeter is the distance or path around a two-dimensional (2-D) shape

pictogram a picture that represents a word or a number

place value the value every digit has in a number, for example, a one, a hundred or a thousand

100s	10s	1s
	5	3

polygon a flat shape with three or more straight sides

predict guess with reasons

prism a solid with two identical ends and flat sides

problem a question to which you have to find the right answer by using mathematics or logical thought

proportion a constant comparison between two numbers or two quantities

puzzle a game or problem

pyramid a solid with a polygon for a base and triangular sides

Q

quadrilateral a 2-D shape that has 4 straight sides

R

ratio a relationship between two amounts; the relationship is shown by using two numbers that tell you how many times bigger or smaller one amount is than the other

reason a cause for an event, or to explain why things happen

reasoning the action of thinking

remainder the amount left over after division

right angle a 90° angle

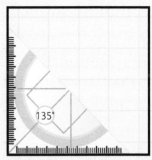

round to make a number simpler, but keep its value close to what it was

S

scale a system according to which things are measured

scale an object that is used to measure weight

sequence a list of numbers in which each number is obtained according to a specific rule

share to divide equally

solution the correct answer to a problem

solve find the answer to

south the direction 180 degrees from north or 90 degrees clockwise from east

square a 2-D shape with 4 sides of equal length and four right angles

square number (or perfect square) is a number that is formed by multiplying the same number with itself, for example 25 is a square number because it is formed by 5 × 5

subtract to take away something from another

subtraction a way of taking one number or amount away from another number or amount

symmetrical each half is exactly the same

symmetry when a straight line can be drawn through an object or shape to divide two parts so that the one side looks like a mirror image of the other

systematic done according to a fixed plan or system

T

table information arranged in rows and columns

take away minus or subtract

tally a score, or mark to show an amount; 卌 |||

ten thousand the product of 100 × 100, or 1 more than 9 999; 10 000

thousand the product of 10 × 100, or 1 more than 999; 1 000

time a measurement of an action or event

times multiply

times table a table showing numbers multiplied together

timetable a chart showing the departure and arrival times; a schedule or program of events with starting and ending times

triangle a 2-D shape with 3 straight sides

turn to rotate or change position

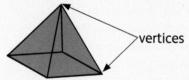

Turn 90° clockwise

V

Venn diagram a diagram with circles to show sets

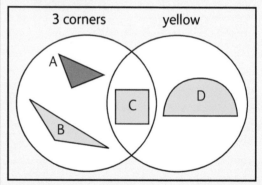

vertical upright, at a right angle to the horizontal

vertices (plural for vertex) the point where two sides or lines meet

vertices

W

weight mass of an object

west the direction a three-quarter turn or 270 degrees from north

width measurement of how far from side to side of an object